Publisher: Linda Wagar
Ottawa, Ontario
Website: www.canadianmarathonstories.ca

Library and Archives Canada Cataloguing in Publication

Canadian marathon stories: a book of extraordinary inspirations / editor, Linda Rainville Wagar.

Includes 4 French stories.

ISBN 978-0-9784204-0-6

    1. Runners (Sports)--Canada--Biography.
    2. Marathon running.
    3. Inspiration.
    I. Wagar, Linda Rainville, 1957

GV1061.14.C35 2007
796.42092'271
C2007-906081-1

www.CanadianMarathonStories.ca

Contents

Histoire en français

French story

"Without the funding that I received from the Canadian Athletes Now Fund, I would not be wearing the gold medal around my neck."

~ *Adam van Koeverden, 2004 Olympic Gold & Bronze Medalist, Kayak, Fund Recipient*

"I can't put into words how important the Canadian Athletes Now Fund was to me and how necessary it is for all of Canada's amateur athletes."

~ *Jayna Hefford, Canadian Olympian, Women's Hockey, Fund Recipient*

"I have witnessed the positive impact that the Canadian Athletes Now Fund has had on many of my teammates. This organization has not only supported athletes financially, but it has raised a tremendous amount of awareness to the importance in sports in Canada!"

~ *David Sabourin, National Team Member Trampoline, Fund Recipient*

"The Canadian Athletes Now Fund has brought the support of Canadian athletes, our "future heroes," to a new level. I have a poster in my classroom that states: "You cannot fulfill your dreams unless you dare to risk it all" the Canadian Athletes Now Fund is helping to fulfill many dreams including my own!"

~ *Mandy Poitras, Cycling, Fund Recipient*

The CAN Fund

Buying this book is choosing to support the Canadian Athletes Now Fund. The CAN Fund is a not-for-profit organization devoted solely to raising funds and awareness for Canada's athletes. The Fund has been set up to help Canada's athletes get ready for international summer and winter Games. Monies donated to the Fund are put directly into the hands of Canadian elite athletes to support their training, coaching, nutrition and living expenses in preparation for international competition. The mission is to underwrite the expenses of as many Canadian athletes as possible, as support is needed years before the medals can be obtained.

· Direct funding is provided to both able-bodied and paralympic athletes.

· Twice a year athletes can apply for funding - spring and fall. With each application athletes must fill out a very detailed assessment of their current training and financial situation.

· The Fund provides approved athletes with $6,000 each, twice a year. Athletes can receive up to $12,000 a year from the Fund.

· Athletes use this direct funding for better nutrition, coaching, training camps, international competitions and basic living expenses.

· In October 2003 the Fund received charitable status.

· CAN Fund was formerly known as "See You In".

· CAN Fund has raised over $4 million, since its inception in 1997.

Foreword
John Stanton

Most sports conclude with a winner and a loser. Marathon running is unique. Success comes from preparation, tenacity and discipline, culminating with a celebration at the finish line. Marathon running is a continual journey of self assessment and improvement.

Runners make marathons a major part of their lives - for the challenge, with generous rewards achieved through a clear focus on a goal. This continual setting of new goals and striving to achieve loftier results is what gives life itself, substance.

Marathon running creates a personal, professional and community win for the athlete.

Runners are all athletes, regardless of their performance prowess. Some are fast, some slow, but they all start at the same start line and finish at the same finish line. The slow runner is amazed by the speed of the elite; the elite are amazed at the staying power of the slower runner.

Some runners run for self satisfaction, others to overcome personal obstacles. Still others, run for people unable to run for themselves.

Children run for the joy of play; adults run to rediscover play.

Performance athletes run for the pride of their country and the accolades of their peers.

Running a marathon is not easy. If it was, everyone would run a marathon to savor the empowerment and joy delivered at the finish line.

The stories in the following pages touch the hot buttons of running. You will be inspired by Mark Black as he recants his journey of insurmountable odds when facing a double lung and heart transplant. You will be stimulated by his complex and ultimate journey to a marathon finish line.

You will be entertained with the brilliant, lively and humorous writings of Louise Rachlis.

Enjoy the splendid photos that capture the power and social aspects of the group run. Marathon running has transformed itself from a solitary, lonely sport to the community connection and support provided through the group run. Each runner benefits from the group dynamics, sharing their great conversations, training tips, nutritional choices, schedule planning and life in general.

Discover destination marathons as Jennifer Sharpe describes the fun of running the Disney Marathon.

The story of Shannon Loutitt will caress you with her heart-rending story of running Boston in the footsteps of her famous grandfather.

Marathon success stories are written by the Canadian community and assembled to assist Canadian athletes. The inspiration and motivation is yours to discover the best within you.

The book is dedicated to Emilie Mondor who, as described by her performance coach Ken Parker, was one of the best up and coming female marathon runners in the world. While her life was tragically cut short, the memory of this very talented athlete will live long in the hearts of Canadians.

Linda Wagar has assembled a charming collection of marathon success stories. Each story shares the true joy and deep meaning of marathon running success.

Read, then re-read these fascinating stories. Discover the athlete within you as you become a runner with a marathon success story to share in the future.

You too can do it and finish smiling!

John Stanton,

President & Founder
The Running Room

This book is dedicated to the memory of Emilie Mondor, Canada's Olympic hopeful in the marathon for Beijing 2008. This book is further dedicated to my marathon hero Terry Fox.

To my husband, Carl, who's support made the dream of this book become reality.

They have taught me to believe that anything is possible.

Linda Rainville Wagar,
Editor

At the age of 43, I decided to learn to run. I needed to find a quick and easy way to stay fit and keep up with my 2 young children. What developed was a love of not only running, but of long distance running. What also ensued was my ability to change aspects of my lifestyle and embrace healthier habits. Two years later, I would enter and complete the New York City marathon. It was a pivotal moment in my life. I returned home, to Ottawa with a mission.

I had always been inspired by running stories. I would give back to the running community by launching a website called "Canadian Marathon Stories". This book is a compilation of some of these stories. I hope they will inspire, motivate, and entertain. This is my labour of love and proceeds from the sale of this book will go to the Canadian Athletes Now Fund, a not-for-profit organization dedicated to raising funds to help support our Canadian athletes.

This book was inspired over the course of many runs. Kilometer after kilometer and many training partners lent me the encouragement, ideas and creativity that I would need to see this project through. There are too many of you to name, but you know who you are and your footprints are on these pages. I look forward to hearing your comments on this book!

Feel free to submit your stories and we will post them on our website.

www.canadianmarathonstories.ca

linda@lindawagar.com

Emilie Mondor
Photo courtesy of Bernard Brault
-LaPresse

Tribute to Emilie Mondor
by
Lynne Bermel

■ *"This book is dedicated to Emilie Mondor - the soft-spoken Mascouche, Quebec native known as much for her infectious love of running as her unparalleled mental toughness"*

Emilie Mondor, 25, one of Canada's most accomplished distance runners, had her marathon dreams cut short when she was killed tragically in a car accident in September 2006. The first Canadian to dip below the 15-minute mark in the 5,000 meters, she had been training in Ottawa for her marathon debut in the ING New York City Marathon. Her death shocked the running community in Canada and around the world.

This book is dedicated to Emilie Mondor - the soft-spoken Mascouche, Quebec native known as much for her infectious love of running as her unparalleled mental toughness. She had represented Canada at the 2004 Olympics in Athens and was looking toward racing the marathon in Beijing in 2008. She had been injured throughout 2005 with a rare bone disease and was on the comeback trail - hoping to translate her international success as a track runner into marathon glory.

But it was not to be. Instead, the women racing the streets of New York City wore black wrist bands in her memory.

Her last coach, Ottawa's Ken Parker, believes that Emilie would have rewritten the record books for marathon running in Canada. Her training and results from testing at the human performance lab in Ottawa just before she died indicated that she could have been one of the best female marathoners in the world.

But it was more than her physical strength...

"Emilie loved to run more than anyone I know," he says. "Some people have the ability to hurt but they just don't have the engine to do it. Emilie had both. She had a very special gift and she lived up to it. She reined in every last ounce of energy from her body every time she raced. She held nothing back. That's what set her apart."

Emilie Mondor, Canadian marathon hopeful, died much too early. If she taught us anything, it was to never give up. To focus on the positive, no matter how bad it gets. And to share the joy and love of running.

Emilie, you touched so many during your short life. We will miss you but we will never forget you.

Lynne Bermel is a former world-ranked Ironman competitor and marathoner. She is currently living in Ottawa as a communications consultant, as well as a freelance writer and TV host. She was one of the last people to interview Emilie Mondor.

Hommage à Emilie Mondor par Linda Rainville Wagar

■ *"Les deux, vous aviez un rêve. Pour toi, Pékin; pour Terry, courir à travers le Canada."*

Je te connaissais grâce aux histoires dans les journaux. Tu étais l'exemple de la détermination, du talent, de l'ambition. Tu avais le focus nécessaire pour atteindre et réaliser ton rêve. C'est ce que je retenais de toi.

Je ne te connaissais pas personnellement mais étant "fan" de course, je t'encourageais de loin. Tu avais aussi relevé des défis, ce qui te rendait encore plus forte. Tu étais unique, la femme la plus rapide au Canada à courir le 5,000 mètres et ce, en moins de 15 minutes! Plus tard, j'ai appris ton départ de ce monde, mais pas avant d'avoir accompli une belle petite course de 29 km avec ton entraineur. Tu te sentais bien.

Le lendemain, quand le monde a appris ton départ de cette vie, je ne pus que proposer à mon groupe qui s'entraînait pour le semi marathon, de courir la distance de 18km en ta mémoire. Souvent, je sens que tu cours avec moi. Tu me donnes cette force, tu m'inspires. Je sais que je ne suis pas seule Émilie, je ne suis pas seule qui cours et qui sens ta présence.

Plus tard, j'ai compris que ce livre te serait dédié à toi, Émilie. Tu représentais les qualités de mon héros Terry Fox. Les deux, vous aviez un rêve. Pour toi, c'était les Olympiques de 2008 à Pékin; pour Terry, c'était courir à travers le Canada. On court maintenant pour vous, pour que vos rêves continuent à nous inspirer à aller de l'avant, parce que l'on peut. Terry Fox, avec son "marathon de l'espoir" et maintenant, avec "la course d'Emilie". Merci pour ce cadeau.

Merci très sincèrement,
Linda Rainville Wagar

■ "One who wants a
rose must respect
the thorn."

~ *Persian Proverb*

Richard Bercuson

■ *"The moment at the finish line is burned into my memory."*

Richard Bercuson from Ottawa, Ontario submitted his whole training, in writing, to our website. In case some of you would prefer to read instead of run, see: www.canadianmarathonstories.ca

Everything about running a marathon was stacked against me. I decided to do it anyway.

I was over 50. I had an affinity for fine food, including potato chips. I'd have to train in the misery known as an Ottawa winter. And I didn't own a pair of cute running tights.

Immune to common sense, I registered for a marathon clinic. Every week I sat in a room with other delusional souls (though they appeared outwardly normal) to learn the finer points of marathon training.

Training for my first marathon changed my life. Rather, it occupied my life. No, it became my life.

At the first session, the instructor pointed to his hand-drawn map of southern Ontario. He explained how 18 weeks hence, our training would cover the approximate distance from Windsor to Ottawa, about 990 km.

There was a whack of syndromes I could suffer from and we were asked if any of us had them. Patellar-femoral syndrome (PFS)? Yes, well no, well just a little when I descended stairs. Did that count?

Iliotibial band strain? Not really. If you don't count when I tried to change direction.

Shin splints? No. Definitely not...actually just once...but it went away.

Tight hams? Just one, the right one. Stubbornly so. Was that an injury or merely a nuisance? There didn't seem to be a sports medicine definition for nuisance.

Plantar fasciitis? Hadn't had that. Besides, any word with so many of the same vowel was best ignored.

Achilles tendonitis? Injured no. Tight yes. Did that mean strained? Did I therefore have a syndrome?

He also mentioned back problems, which could be related to hip problems or knee problems or ankle problems. I was taking the garbage down the stairs one day, gingerly placing each foot on each lower step knowing my PFS might act up. My wife was watching me. At that moment, my toes touched the stair. A pain shot up from my patella, traversed the sartorius, danced across the gracilis, bounced along the rectus femoris, and pinged into my vastus lateralis, all in a millisecond. My knee buckled slightly as the garbage bag swayed into the staircase opening and hovered over the dog's head.

"Marathon, eh?" she grumbled.

"I'm fine," I winced. "Everyone gets these things. It's just a syndrome."

With that, I took out the garbage. Painfully.

Otherwise, my training went smoothly. The learning curve was steep. I trained with a group comprised mostly of women, not exactly a hardship. Once, I overheard a comment about female hygiene. I remember turning my head slightly, to which one of the ladies joked, "Look Richard, that's the risk of running with a bunch of women. Pretty soon, you're going to start ovulating."

By race day, I was a nervous wreck, afraid a syndrome would overtake me.

The finish line was a little higher than I expected, about two inches above ground level. For a moment, I wasn't sure I'd get over it seeing as how I wasn't watching for the line. During the last 50 meters – that's 42,150 meters from the

12

Start! – I extended both arms skyward, cap clenched in one hand, and my mouth etched into a semblance of a smile.

As my moment approached, the cheering crowds along both sides of the road obliterated what was left of my concentration. By then, the thighs were tight and sapped. The calves had long since bought the farm. Both knees had been revolting since the 32 K mark and threatened to do nasty things to my upper body, like buckle me in half. My shoulders ached so badly that lifting my arms actually came as a great relief.

Just before breaking into my "Look at me – I've done it!" trot, I noticed I was alone, completely and utterly by myself running towards that all too high line. This was a solo act. Slow or fast, smartly-trained or not, fed or empty, hydrated or dry, muscles primed or lazy, I was about to accomplish something entirely by myself.

It came down to me and me alone. Me and my shoes and my tight hamstring and the chocolate gels and orange Gatorade and bits of energy food my wife called "snackie-poos". Me and the cool max shirt and the liberally applied body glide and the new socks.

The moment at the finish line is burned into my memory. Exhausted, hurting, hungry, dizzy, I shortened my steps.

Slow...slow...I lifted my right thigh as high as it could go. Fortunately, that was two and half inches up, giving me a full half inch clearance over the rubber mat. I planted my right foot on the mat and instructed the left foot that it was now okay to seek flat ground on the other side.

Ping! Sonuvagun, I just ran a marathon.

Richard is a writer and high school teacher who has since run other marathon and half marathon races. He is a columnist for the Ottawa Citizen, and Monitor, a computer magazine. He is an award-winning short story author and playwriter. When not running, he coaches hockey, and he is an instructor, for Canada's national coaching program. He has thoroughly searched his family tree and still can`t find a genealogical link to ancient Greek runners.

■ Be realistic.
Plan for a miracle.

~ Bhagwan Shree
Rajneesh

Karen Beitel

■ *"As I lay shivering, the firemen arrive... then the ambulance... then the doctors..."*

Success is sometimes not measured by crossing a finish line. Karen Beitel, from Toronto Ontario knows there is always another Boston. Fortunately for all runners, there are always other races.

It was a hot day in Hopkinton, Massachusetts.

This was the Boston Marathon. The projected forecast was clear skies, with a high of 85 degrees. The heat intimidated everyone, even the Kenyans. The lines at the port-o-potties never ended as the bladders of 20,000 runners worked furiously to get rid of excess fluid. The communal nerves didn't help much either. Despite the difficulties I was about to face, my spirits soared.

The gun went off and the race began. "Slowly," I said to myself, "Take it out slowly." I knew it was going to be a tough day, especially considering that the hottest day of my training was on a spring day in Saskatchewan. After the first 5K, I stopped at the water station. "Have a drink. Take in some fluid," my 'inside voice' said. I followed its advice and high-fived the kids who lined the route, the greatest fans ever. At Mile 6, the heat got to me and trouble began.

My 'inside voice' asked, "Mile 6? How are you ever going to get to mile 26.2? You haven't even reached 1/4 of the distance!" I looked around, saw some railway tracks, and spoke back, "Well, if I don't make it to the end, I'll take a train back to Boston."

I ran one mile at a time. Mile 7. Ugh. Mile 8. Ugh. Mile 9. Ugh. All the while I kept drinking Gatorade and water. Finally I came upon Mile 13.1. "Halfway there!" I thought with great relief. The 'inside voice' continued, "If all else fails, you can probably just walk back to Boston." The voice was definitely more positive than earlier. I high-five a few more fans (who informed me the Red Sox beat the Yankees) and carried on.

Then at Mile 16 I faced the famous Newton Hills, 5 miles of rolling terrain climaxing at Heart Break Hill. The battle continued, but my stomach took on emotions of its own: NAUSEA! The 'inside voice' grew more and more aggressive, repeating three words over and over again, "I feel sick! I feel sick! I feel sick!" It was so loud that at Mile 20, I pulled over at the Red Cross First Aid Tent. "I feel sick," I said aloud to an attendant. She passed me a bag and I vomited.

I wasn't alone. I was in the company of many fellow runners, some feeling worse than me. One of them (his accent clearly identified him as a Boston local), having his leg massaged, looked up at me and said, "We' a gonna do it, no matta what, we' a gonna finish this race." Then he offered me some advice, "Try and pee. It might make you feel better." I tried; I felt better.

I started running again.

I arrived at the top of Heart Break Hill surprised that the hills were over. Mile 21. Only 2 more miles until I would see my friends, Raymond and Tracy, who were strategically placed at Mile 23 to give me a push to the finish line. "Just try and get there," my 'inside voice' prodded. After what seemed like an eternity, I saw my two friends - beacons on Beacon St.

"Walk with me for a bit," my 'outside' voice pleaded with them. As they accompanied me along the street, the heat again became overwhelming. My stomach again encouraged me to the side, where I threw-up for a second time.

The man in a hat could have been a fireman, or a police officer. "Ma'am, the Red Cross First Aid Tent is right back there" he said. I look back from where I had come and resolutely replied, "I'm not going back."

We walked on.

Then, my nemesis appeared at Mile 24 in the guise of another Red Cross First Aid Centre. I pulled off the course and had a seat. The attendants took my blood pressure and told me to stay as long as I'd like, until finally a doctor said to me, "I recommend you not finish this race." Suddenly the 'inside voice' disappeared.

It was over. I was not going to make it to the finish line, only 2 miles away. It was the longest 2 miles I ever experienced. I vomited for the 3rd and final time. The doctors rushed over, laid me down and jabbed an I.V. into my arm. Then they placed the 911 call.

As I lay shivering, the firemen arrive... then the ambulance... then the doctors...

At the end of the day, there I was at St. Elizabeth Hospital where I lay for 3 hours with a broken heart. I never finished the Boston Marathon. But the 'inside voice' is back, "There's always another Boston. Let's try again next year."

Karen Beitel - Yonge/Eglinton Running Room store. Last year she requalified for the Boston Marathon and is registered for the 2008 race.

■ Don't ask for an easier life. Ask to be a stronger person.

~ *Anonymous*

Mark Black

This story is from Mark Black, of Moncton, New Brunswick. His second chance at life, takes him places he never dreamed possible. The gift of generosity is priceless. This story is why each of us might consider signing organ donation cards.

■ *"Almost hurricane conditions, the winds were 70km/h!"*

It would be the perfect ending to a miraculous journey. Running the marathon would prove everything that I'd wanted people to believe was true. Anything was possible.

Three years before I lined up on that start line, I was lying in a hospital bed, dying. After battling a congenital heart disease for 22 years, my heart was on its last legs...!

In May 2001, my doctor said the words that changed my life, "You need a heart-double lung transplant and you need it now... or you won't live to see your 25th birthday."

I moved away from my family and moved to Toronto to wait for a transplant. I waited for ten months, six of them in a hospital bed, but I was lucky.

In September 2002, I received "The Gift of Life", and since that day, I haven't looked back.

So when I drove to Halifax to run the Bluenose International Marathon in May 2005 I was confident that I could do it. Confident, until I woke up on race day.

When I looked out the window of my hotel room that morning, I couldn't believe my eyes. It was raining... sideways. Almost hurricane conditions, the winds were 70km/h!

There were doubts that the marathon would even happen. The start was delayed for over an hour as race organizers scrambled to reset pylons and water stations that had blown over the night before and re-routed the course to avoid the bridge that was no longer safe to cross in the wind.

After waiting around for an hour the race got under way. Immediately we were faced with the challenge of a VERY STRONG headwind. Although I know it isn't possible, it seemed like we ran into the wind the whole run.

As I approached the 21K mark of what was now a double-loop course, I was seriously tempted to exit the course, collect a 1/2 marathon medal and call it a day... but I kept running.

At about 28K I pulled a Clark Kent. That's what I like to call it. I was running along the streets of Halifax when my parents, who were there for moral support following me in a car to stay warm and dry, pulled up beside me. "Get in!" they shouted. I felt a little bit like I was being abducted. I jumped in the car and inside was an extra shirt, jacket, new mittens and a hat. I had been freezing as the pouring rain had soaked through my jacket and the wind was seemingly blowing right through me.

As quickly as I could (my hands were too cold to have much dexterity) I took off my wet clothes and put on the dry ones. Thanking my parents, I got out of the car, stepped back into the storm and kept running.

My new warm duds refreshed me and I ran well until about 33 or 34K. I remember running on Lower Water St in Halifax, looking out at the grey ocean, and I felt the motivation - the little bit that was left- drain from me. I looked ahead of me and I couldn't see a soul (there weren't a lot of spectators in that kind of weather). I looked behind me and I couldn't see anyone. I realized that if I stopped right there, no one needed to know.

As my trot slowed to a walk I contemplated quitting, flirted with the idea for a few minutes, then I looked at my hand. On my hand I'd written the names of friends that I'd made waiting for a transplant who hadn't been as fortunate as me.

They died WAITING for a transplant because there weren't enough donors in Canada to find them a match in time. After that quick dose of perspective I realized how fortunate I was just to be alive and breathing. I HAD to finish this race. I certainly didn't have a good excuse to stop now.

After 5hrs and 16min (about 45min slower than my goal time) I finished my first marathon. It was, as it is for everyone, an amazing experience. Conquering that challenge was awesome, and to know all that I'd had to overcome to get there made it even better.

Today I still think about that day. I've run other races but I think that one will always be the sweetest. It proved to me, and hopefully to others that anything is possible.

Mark Black has completed his third marathon. He now works as an Inspirational Speaker speaking to schools, corporations and associations across North America. To learn more about Mark's services, go to:

www.MarkBlackSpeaks.com

Pierre Bourassa

■ *"Il y avait même au 30e km un vin blanc froid servi avec des moules! Mais attention! On nous servait un fond de verre, équivalant à deux gorgées; et je m'empressais de caler ensuite un bon verre d'eau. "*

Pierre Bourassa de St. Paul-de-Montminy, dans les Appalaches, est à la retraite. Il est passionné de la course: 112 marathons (15 en 8 mois en 2006!) 5 fois le 100K, entre autres. Il est membre du Club Les Vainqueurs de Montréal. Le travail pratiquement bénévole qu'il fait pour les coureurs à titre d'organisateur de voyages le tient pas mal occupé. L'histoire de son marathon en France démontre le côté social qui se développe chez le marathonien. Moi, ça me tente de m'embarquer!

"Nous reviendrons l'an prochain." C'est ce que nous avions promis, Alain Bélanger, Jean-Paul Bourgeault et moi, aux amis français rencontrés en septembre 1990. Promesse tenue! Aux trois "récidivistes" se joignirent 10 autres pour ce qui s'avéra la plus originale expérience de course à vie.

Le 11 septembre 1991, nous étions accueillis à l'aéroport Charles-de-Gaulle par Denise et Yves Seigneuric du Club Moussy-le-Neuf. Nous avons été pris en charge par les membres et amis du Club pour la nuit, et le lendemain, avec nos véhicules loués, nous prenions la route très tôt, pour éviter l'heure de pointe sur le périphérique de Paris.

Destination: Bordeaux, pour un séjour de 3 jours dans la région. C'est que le 14 septembre avait lieu la 7e édition du Marathon des Châteaux du Médoc, considéré "le plus beau marathon au monde", aussi qualifié de "plus long au monde". Plus beau, parce que son parcours passe à travers les vignobles les plus beaux du monde, et parce que les milliers de coureurs déguisés et les 20,000 spectateurs et bénévoles contribuent à lui donner une atmosphère de fête; plus long, parce que les tables de victuailles à tous les 2.5 km et surtout les 7 points officiels (à part des autres non officiels) de dégustation de vin sont responsables de quelques zigzags supplémentaires à travers les vignes!

Il faut dire que les dégustations avaient commencé l'avant-veille avec la visite du fameux petit village de Saint-Émilion, et la veille avec celle du château de Maucaillou, de son Musée du Vin et de ses caves. La collecte des dossards à Pauillac, lieu de départ du marathon, fut assez "joyeuse", mais pas autant que le souper "Mille-Pâtes" au château Pontet-Canet sous un immense chapiteau: c'est là que 1,500 marathoniens et amis trinquèrent et festoyèrent jusque très tard le soir.

La nuit fut très courte, et le réveil fut très pénible. Mais tout notre groupe se présenta à la ligne de départ du marathon. Nous n'étions pas déguisés, mais il fallait voir l'accoutrement de certains coureurs, l'un déguisé en évêque, d'autres en schtroumpfs tout bleus. Il y avait le cortège de Blanche-Neige avec ses sept nains, une diligence plein de cow-boys tirant sur des Indiens simulant une attaque avec des flèches... Et ces coureurs faisaient tout le parcours, costumés ainsi!

J'ai couru le marathon aux côtés d'un ami, François Lauzé. Je m'étais promis de faire la fête, et je peux vous dire que je n'ai pas manqué aucune table de ravitaillement ni aucun point de dégustation de vin, au grand dam de mon ami: "on ne finira jamais, qu'il disait"... Il y avait même au 30e km un vin blanc froid servi avec des moules! Mais attention! On nous servait un fond de verre, équivalant à deux gorgées; et je m'empressais de caler ensuite un bon verre d'eau. Je l'ai quand même terminé en 4h14, ce marathon... avec quelques crampes, je l'avoue!

Il fallait voir le cérémonial entourant la présentation du vin: après qu'on ait franchi les portes du domaine (certains vignobles n'ouvrent qu'à cette occasion du marathon), un serveur bien accoutré, avec serviette blanche sur le bras, vous présente une sélection de vins devant une petite table sur laquelle sont disposées de belles coupes. Et vous faites votre choix. J'ai été pris en flagrant délit, une coupe à la main, par un photographe officiel du journal Jogging International, à mon insu.

Certains d'entre nous ont eu des mésaventures sur le parcours.
Monique St-Cyr est restée longtemps embarrée dans une toilette privée assez éloignée du chemin: le loquet extérieur s'est refermé; une dame alertée par ses cris est venue à son secours. Un autre s'est fait frapper par une auto: il ne s'est pas soucié que le bénévole arrêtait les coureurs pour faire passer les autos, au lieu du contraire! Et Charles Lacroix de Thetford Mines a eu maille à partir avec un policier et un cycliste: il a été renversé par le cycliste et s'est retrouvé sous le vélo, la moustache dans les rayons de roue et les lacets dans l'engrenage, le cycliste par-dessus; le policier à qui il demandait de l'aide était plié en deux, mort de rire!

En somme, un marathon à ne pas prendre au sérieux, dans l'esprit même des clubs Spiridon français: "la perf', d'accord; la fête, d'abord!" A preuve, chaque finissant recevait une bouteille de vin à l'arrivée! N'empêche que le premier l'a terminé en 2:23:44. Ah! Quand même!

Dans ses temps libres, Pierre rénove sa 4ième maison centenaire. Dans ces mots, "J'ai comme principe de vivre et de laisser vivre. J'essaie de répandre autour de moi l'harmonie, le respect et l'attention aux autres. C'est dans ces valeurs que je me sens bien."

Rob Bryce at 19KM

Rob Bryce at 40KM

Rob Bryce

■ *"I did not care as all I had to do was follow the person in front of me. "*

Rob Bryce from Prince George BC is a goal setter. His approach is disciplined, he doesn't eat too much, and getting sick before a marathon can happen.

I had been running 5-10 km 3 days a week during my lunch hour with a group of runners for the past couple of years as a way of staying in shape. I had never had any ambition to run a marathon until one day, discussion during one of our runs was about a couple of my co-runners and their marathon plans for the year. Eventually, I would find myself at a Marathon in Red Deer, Alberta.

I bought a new pair of running shoes and followed a plan for 3 ½ months. As I increased my mileage each week I went through pain in almost every part of my legs from my feet to shin splints, knees and groin.

The week before the race I was feeling relatively healthy. I had lost 20lbs over the past 6 months while training with only a nagging groin pain when all of a sudden I awoke 4 days before the race with a sore throat. I thought why this, why me and why now. I decided that the training and time I had put in was not going to stop me from running regardless of how I felt.

The day before the race I started to feel better. The sore throat had subsided and I actually felt excited again about running. That evening we attended the pre race pasta party. At our table three guys sat down and introduced themselves and mentioned that they were all running the marathon. During dinner they filled their plates with twice as much food as myself and they all have 3 - 6 desserts each. I thought to myself - am I doing something wrong here by not filling my face with as much food before the race? I had assumed that because one guy had run 6 marathons the previous year and the other had run 4 or 5 in his life, that they were experienced runners and they knew best about the pre-race meal sizes. I decided to just eat my average portion of pasta and see what happened. The evening speaker was an inspiring local runner.

At the start line I positioned my self back about 1/3 way into the 1100 marathon running pack. Once the horn went I said to myself "This is it". "This is what I had been working towards for the last 3 months".

I felt good the first 5 km and had to really slow myself down as I thought my ultimate goal pace was between 5:00 - 5:30 per km. The race course was absolutely brilliant with most of the race along paths beside the Red Deer River. We crossed the river 4 or 5 times throughout the race and this disoriented me a bit. I did not care as all I had to do was follow the person in front of me.

The km's kept ticking off and I passed my wife who was cheering me on for the 2nd time at km 19. It was at this point the half marathon people veered off to the finish line.

Now there were only 300 of us running the next part of the course. I was getting the hang of drinking at the water stops and I took a couple of Power Gels which seemed to give me a boost. We hit a dirt trail that winded through the forest. This section was identical to the trails where I did the majority of my training runs.

I continued to run well until about 34 km. After this point the pain in my legs and the general exhaustion started to take over. I continued to pass the occasional person but my pace had slowed from 5:30 to 5:45 km. I knew I was still going to finish but there was nothing I could do to go any faster.

I saw my wife one more time at the 40 km mark. She later said I did not look like the same runner who had passed her two times earlier in the race.

The last km had a huge hill before a short downhill to the finish line. One guy passed me going up the hill like he had just started the race. I was wondering where he found all the energy to race up this long grinding hill.

I turned the corner and sprinted to the finish line in a time of 3:37:46 (55 out of 300). A finisher's medal was put over my head and a bottle of water put into my hand. My wife and her friend were there to greet me and take a few pictures. All I wanted to do was drink the water and stretch the soreness out of my legs. I was extremely happy with my time although I would have been happy just finishing. I had no idea what to expect or how my body and legs would react to running this far.

Overall it was a great experience for my first marathon. I have not decided whether I will run another one in the future. I am sure if you asked me this question in the last 10km of the race I would say no. I do think that for anyone who has some casual running experience it is a great goal to set and have some fun attaining it.

Rob has gone on to run another marathon, in 3:30. He is passionate about hiking and is the author of a book on hiking trails in North Central B.C. He is an avid fisherman and in the winter he participates in a different type of racing. He and his wife have a kennel of 20 Siberian huskies and they train for sleddog races. He believes his marathon training has helped him be quite successful in this sport.

■ There is no
education like
adversity.

~ *Benjamin Disraeli*

Monica Chokley

I love this story, from Trenton, Ontario. Monica describes accessories, in a way that women can relate; actually, men too.

■ *"I can almost hear Billy Crystal whispering in my ear, "You look marvellous."*

Fitness. I needed fitness. Things were getting a little thick around the middle. "Try running", a dear friend told me, "it costs nothing but a pair of sneakers." I had sneakers, I could do this. A slow start at first, but before I knew it, the sport had me hooked.

But what about the dollar cost? I look back at my second marathon, just run a few days ago. I did a bit of tallying.

The marathon fees are about the same. I missed the cheap fee deadlines, and was stuck with paying $80.

I took a good look at my worn out shoes, gone flat like an old bottle of pop. These new ones are springy and clean and carry a price tag of $140. Can't go cheap; good shoes are a runner's best friend.

Pulling out the old shorts, I realized they were just that: old shorts. Surely I can't run a race as great and mighty as a marathon in these old things. And the new ones out there! Wow, they are lighter than air, with a zippered pocket in the back for gels or an mp3 player. Those are the ones to be wearing when burning up the local roads. Cost of these wonder shorts? A mere $50. Not bad, considering how many miles they will carry me.

Lucky me, over the past two seasons I had collected a few new "technical" shirts from races (there's one bonus for paying those sign up fees). This one will do. But

I can't possibly wear it to the marathon on the off chance that other runners will be wearing the same shirt. I don't want to melt in with the crowd that badly. I like this new shirt, to go with the hot shorts, $30.

I'm almost geared up, except for socks. As a runner I know it's really all about the feet: keep them happy, they'll keep me running, a deal at $11. They have a fancy logo on the ankle, makes me look like a pro. Maybe it'll even help me run faster.

At the running store, I see a wall of nylon caps and visors. The choice overwhelms me. I try on about 200 before deciding on a perfect blue and white cap, $22. Ouch. I'm quick to remind myself of the many miles it will see me through.

There is one more clothing item that needs updating in my wardrobe. The much hated but even more needed running bra. Am I to ask the only person working in the store for bra advice, that guy who looks like he doesn't shave yet standing behind the counter? I. Don't. Think. So. I can figure it out myself. Two hours and 40 bras later, I have found my new best friend: a Champion 36C compression bra. I hand the new-to-shave sales boy my VISA to cover the $45 cost. I'm geared up for this marathon now. The tally: 80+140+50+30+11+22+45=$378.

I had forgotten about 4 gels at a cost of $1.75 each make $7. Inconsequential. A bottle of Gatorade:$1.50. These things need a place to live. I get a fuel belt. A beauty with a Velcro closure for only $40. Costs so far: $378+7+1.50+40=$426.50.

As I stand at the start line, I can almost hear Billy Crystal whispering in my ear, "You look marvellous". And so I do... I stand up taller, pull my hat down lower over my eyes. I am a runner.

My road partner turns to me and grins as we hit the mats at the start line. We've been training for this run all winter. Some days it took a lot of character to get out there in the bitter cold, but we persevered. That's what running does for you; it builds you up to the point where you are willing to try. After awhile, trying is no longer the goal; it's conquering the distance, the elements, and the daily life that tries to hold you back. And we will conquer this marathon.

The first half we chat like we usually do, and sometimes listen to conversations around us. At the 30k mark, I come to the realization that a marathon isn't so much a test of how far one can run, but a mind game. My brain tells my legs to keep it going, left foot, right foot. I look over at my co-runner, I can see he's hurting as much as me. We endure, picking off the kilometres, one at a time.

We count down the last 500 meters. With 150 to go, he says it like I knew he would: "Wanna sprint?"

I search my inner being to see if there is anything left. I reach deep and find it and my legs move faster. "Smile for the camera" I tell him. My foot pounds the mat as I reach the finish. The euphoria I feel washes away the pain. At this point, I don't care what the VISA Company wants from me. It doesn't matter that my shoes are wearing thin and will need replacing again. I learned that the pride and thrill of conquering a marathon cannot be bought for any dollar amount. Right now, I feel like the richest person in the world.

Monica Chokley is a full time student preparing for a career in fitness and health. She is a wife and mother of three. 0600 has become her favourite time of day, running the quiet streets and solving the world's problems.

Nathalie Collin

■ "Le progrès
est impossible
sans changement,
et ceux qui ne
peuvent jamais
changer d'avis ne
peuvent ni changer
le monde ni se
changer
eux-mêmes."

~ *George
Bernard
Shaw*

Nathalie Collin

■ *"Lorsque l'on m'a mis la médaille au cou je suis redescendue sur terre comme lorsqu'on attache un bateau au quai pour ne plus qu'il soit porté par la vague. Mon coeur s'est alors serré: je me rendais compte que j'avais réussi et que l'entraînement avait porté fruit. "*

Nathalie Collin de Montréal, Québec nous raconte avec passion le cheminement de son premier parcours avec cette distance. Elle nous fait apprécier son challenge avec le portrait qu'elle peint.

Courir dans les rues de la belle Chicago!

Enfin j'y étais! Le grand jour était venu et c'est sous le charme de cette grande ville que j'ai couru mon premier marathon. Et quel événement se retrouver parmi quelques 38000 coureurs en ce beau matin ensoleillé mais venteux (on ne la nomme pas la ville des vents pour rien). Le vent est donc chez lui à Chicago.

Tout ce beau monde fébrile attendait avec impatience le coup du départ. Ce dernier s'est déroulé, en dépit de la grande foule sans aucune anicroche. Quelques minutes à peine et le tapis du chronomètre était traversé. Dans cette marée humaine j'avais l'impression d'être une goutte dans l'océan. Tant de gens qui partagent la même passion dans un même endroit! Wow! Qui aurait cru que certains matins je me retrouve seul à frapper du pied sur le trottoir. J'étais fasciné par la sérénité qui m'envahissait. Je constatais que tous ces gens portaient en eux le même désir, franchir le 42ième km.

Une foule plus nombreuse que le peloton, nous accompagnait tout le long du parcours. C'est par la ferveur des spectateurs que je me suis laissée porter.

Le parcours sur lequel nous courions était tout à fait sublime. Les quartiers visités étaient tous plus beaux les un que les autres. Certains quartiers résidentiels impressionnaient de par l'architecture de ces immeubles et était encadré par de majestueux arbres qui recouvraient la rue, donnant l'impression de nous faire l'accolade. Certes nous courions dans des quartiers plus pauvres mais c'est, de se côté, la chaleur humaine de ces résidents qui est venu rehausser l'attrait de leur quartier. Le quartier chinois accueillait les coureurs avec le traditionnel dragon. Le sourire et l'enthousiasme étaient au rendez-vous. Des gens venus de partout encourageaient les leurs, ainsi que les inconnus.

Mon expérience fut tellement agréable que je n'ai pas senti les kilomètres s'accumuler et ce n'est qu'au 40e km que le vent cinglant est venu refroidir ma candeur. Curieusement, près de deux km de la fin je voyais des gens s'arrêter pour s'étirer et marcher. J'ai vu quelques visages en questionnements... Je me suis alors dit: Je ne suis plus bien loin, j'ai froid, mes muscles sont raidis par celui-ci mais bon dieu que je suis contente! Soudain la course semblait longue. Le fil d'arriver c'est enfin pointé. J'ai passé ce dernier en 3h40 et 58s. Mes pieds ne touchaient plus le sol. À ce moment là j'avais le coeur et le pied léger. Lorsque l'on m'a mis la médaille au cou je suis redescendu sur terre comme lorsqu'on attache un bateau au quai pour ne plus qu'il soit porté par la vague. Mon coeur s'est alors serré. Je réalisais que j'avais réussi et que l'entraînement avait porté fruit. Deux mois et demi d'entraînement spécifique et déjà la fin du marathon. Deux larmes ont coulé sur mes joues. Mon vécu, l'ombre et la lumière m'ont guidés jusqu'au fil d'arrivée.

Nathalie Collin est née à Montréal et y vit également. Dans la vie, elle est animalière et gère une animalerie. À l'aube de l'an 2000 un ami et elle ont fondé le site courir.org pour pallier au manque de sites québécois renfermant de l'information sur la course à pied. À ce jour, le site compte près de 4 000 abonnés et le site connait un nombre de visites continuellement en hausse. Toujours à la direction du site, Nathalie et son ami continuent leur mission qui est d'informer les gens sur la course à pied et en faire connaître les bienfaits.

www.courir.org

Mark & Amanda Collis

Running is simple. You put your shoes on and go. For these runners, from Burlington Ontario, it is father and daughter time. This duo share incomparable memories.

■ *"I run with Amanda for only two reasons. First and foremost we run together because Amanda enjoys it and secondly, I run with her because I can. "*

Why do we do what we do? I guess I really should say, "Why I do what I do." I can't speak for Amanda and she can't explain it to you in words.

First off, let me tell you a little bit about Amanda. She is our middle child and she was born in 1985 with cerebral palsy that affects her speech and muscle control. She is pretty much confined to her wheelchair and has to have constant care. Amanda is also developmentally challenged, but she seems to be unaware she's handicapped and she behaves like a happy, mischievous little kid.

I run because I like the personal challenge of racing, the camaraderie of fellow runners and the feeling of movement that it brings. It's a liberation of body, mind and spirit that makes me feel better about myself and those around me. It gives me a chance to be both student and teacher, to motivate and be motivated by other athletes. I run because I enjoy it. I'm not terribly fast, but then running for most of us is more than just about finishing first.

Why do I run with Amanda? I do it because I like doing things with my children and running is something that I can share with her. I do not feel that I'm doing anything special at all. For me, it's really not a big deal, it's just time spent with my family.

When I found out that Amanda likes to go running, it gave me an activity that we could both enjoy together. She gets out of her wheelchair for a while and enjoys the sun and fresh air, the attention of others and ice cream after our usual Wednesday night summer runs. I get to spend some solo time with my middle daughter.

Amanda likes to go running, but she likes to go racing even more. If I am racing solo, I can't let her see me

2006
FOREST CITY MARATHON
LONDON, ONTARIO

wearing the running club singlet, because she gets upset if she thinks I'm going without her. She is generally pretty quiet on the road, she's overloaded with stimuli, but at home before the run, it's a sing-song chorus of "DA-AD!", tap-tap-taping on her wrist ("Is it time to go?") and squeals of excitement when she sees her racing stroller. You wouldn't have to ask if she liked running if you saw her then.

I'm not looking for attention, fame or fortune. Neither are we a side show for people to gawk at or feel sorry for. None of this is our style. There are other reasons for running together, like raising the visibility of the handicapped in our community and bringing attention to their inclusion into every day activities, but these aren't the real reasons we do it. I run with Amanda for only two reasons. First and foremost we run together because Amanda enjoys it and secondly, I run with her because I can.

I'd like to say there was a higher ideal or something nobler that motivates me, but I'd be lying to you if I did. It really is nothing all that extraordinary.

I do know that even if Amanda isn't telling her side of the story with words that she can't express, her smile, her eyes and her reactions speak more than loud enough. If you asked and she could talk, I think she would tell you that she runs with her dad simply because it's fun.

Amanda and Mark Collis are a fixture in the Hamilton/Burlington Ontario area running scene and have been participating in races from 5 to 50 kilometres since 2000. They have had the honour and pleasure of qualifying and running in the prestigious Boston Marathon with their heroes, Rick and Dick Hoyt in 2004 and 2005.

More of Mark's essay's on running and the active lifestyle can be read at www.ontherun.ca.

Tina Connelly

Photos courtesy of
NYRR Club

Tina & Brendan
Connelly
www.strong-women.com

Brendan Connelly

■ *"At mile 22 ...it happened, suddenly my legs cramped up, I got dizzy and was struggling to keep my stride. "*

Elite runners are regular people with exceptional talent. Brendan Connelly from Port Coquitlam British Columbia, reports this marathoner's story with much pride. It speaks volumes about the talent this country has.

This story is about my wife's marathon debut. Like most distance runners, she downplays her achievements.

In her first half marathon attempt in a long time, she won the America's Finest City ½ Marathon in San Diego, CA on a hilly course in 1:14. Given that time, she thought she might attempt the full marathon. She chose the California International Marathon in Sacramento, CA. She came in second place in a time of 2:34:44, which was good for $3000 US.

The following is a copy of an e-mail that Tina received from her friend, you might as well get it from the source...Later, I will tell you my story.

"Tina,

All I have to say is...F***ing awesome!

Cheers, Sarah"

"Sarah,

Thanks for the note. Here is how it all happened...I started off conservatively, which is not something I'm very good at but I'm working on. I was running in 4th for the first ten miles at 5:40/mile pace. I was cruising on at 2:29 marathon pace and it felt easy!!! At mile ten, I moved into second place with the Mexican girl running with me until mile 15, where she dropped off. I went through the half at about 1:14:40. Miles were still clicking by at a consistent 5:41. At mile 20, where I was told most marathoners "Hit the Wall", I still felt invincible! However, I was having trouble drinking out of the small paper cups throughout the race. I was going to run 2:29 and get the Olympic standard. I was also closing in on the Australian girl who ended up winning in 2:29:21 (course record). At mile 22...it happened, suddenly my legs cramped up, I got dizzy and was struggling to keep my stride. I think I slowed down to 7 min. miles by then and it was all I could do to finish! Basically, I jogged across the line and as soon as I stopped, I blacked out and collapsed. All I could hear were muffled voices (like Charlie Brown's parents and teachers, you know, "Woh, woh, woh") and someone yelling, "Get a wheelchair". I always see the medical tents at races and think to myself, "Look at those poor bastards!" Well, that was me. The last 4 miles were probably the worst experience of my running career! Tina, the marathon geek"

...And now the race from my perspective.

I was trying to see the race, from as many vantage points as possible. I was getting the split time between when the leader went by and when Tina passed.

When Tina passed by me at 10 miles, the Australian had a 1:55 lead. Tina was right beside a Mexican and a Russian was about 10 meters back. She looked good and even smiled and waved to me as I cheered for her. She has never waved to me before. In the shorter faster races, she is just too focused.

The next viewing location was at the halfway point. The Russian girl had dropped off and Tina was a stride or two ahead of the Mexican.

My next stop was at 20 1/2 miles. This is where some people start hitting the wall. By this point the Mexican had dropped off from Tina's pace. The Australian looked like she was slowing down a bit and Tina had cut her lead down to 1:40 when they passed me. Then, as you know from her story, she "Bonked".

It was pretty freaky after she crossed the line and just went limp. I felt kinda helpless being on the other side of a fence, not being able to do anything for her. She's always so strong, so it was very tough seeing her like that. I managed to make my way to the medical tent, and saw that Tina was not alone. She felt embarrassed that she had to get wheeled away, but I have total respect for people like that who can push themselves to their extreme limits.

At first she was a little bummed with her time because she was on pace and was so close to getting an Olympic standard before she ran out of gas. She said "I'll never run one of those again" but later that night, after she felt better and had some time to realize how fast she had actually run, she was thinking: "With some more experience and proper fuelling during the race, I could do really well at this distance".

Just to give you an idea of how fast Tina's time was, here are some little trivia tid-bits. Only two Americans have run faster than Tina's time this year. It is easily the fastest time in Canada this year. The next fastest time by a Canadian is 2:36:19. It puts her at 12th in the All Time Canadian Rankings.

There was a quote in the paper from an elite level, local guy from Sacramento who was also in his debut marathon. I guess he had a similar experience as Tina, hitting the wall late in the race but managing to hang on and finish 7th in 2:17 and qualifying for the US Olympic trials. When asked if he thought that the marathon was as tough as he expected, he said, "It's a thousand times tougher! Believe the hype!"

Brendan Connelly, inspired by his wife, has now run his own marathon. Tina Connelly's successes include:
8 time National Champion on Track, Roads & Cross Country.
1999 Pan AM Games 10,000 M Bronze Medal, 2000 Sydney Olympics,10,000 M 19th heat 1, 2001 Francophone Games, 5,000 M Gold Medal.,2001 World Track & Field Championships,10,000 M 20th, Marathon, 33rd. 2004 World Cross Country Championships (Team Bronze) 2005 World Half-Marathon Championships 39th.

Robert Davidson

Robert Davidson

■ *"… et soudaine- ment, c'est plein de gens et full animation! Des coureurs, des cyclistes, des patineurs. C'est l'anarchie, et j'adore!"*

Il y aura un marathon pour la première fois en plus de 12 ans à Montréal en 2003. L'auteur, Robert Davidson, espère que ce sera l'occasion de réunir enfin les marathoniens locaux. Or il n'y rencontrera que solitude et désolation sous un soleil implacable… jusqu' à ce que…

Déjà aux aurores on savait que la journée allait être cuisante au max! Une chaleur caniculaire qui allait certainement nous ralentir, mais je ne prenais pas cette course au sérieux. En effet, j'avais couru le Marathon de Québec deux semaines avant…

Le marathon de Montréal allait surtout avoir le mérite de reconstituer la diaspora des marathoniens Montréalais qui doivent courir ailleurs, comme à Québec, New York, Chicago, Boston, car il n'y a pas eu de marathon ici depuis 13 ans.

Les coureurs sont une espèce grégaire

Ce n'est pas tout le monde qui trouve qu'il est sage de courir deux marathons en deux semaines, mais j'espérais que Louise Voghel, qui nous avait montré un superbe chrono de 3 heures pile à Québec, vienne faire un tour.

Est-ce qu'on verra Sylvie Watts? Roger Cool? Sheila Foley? Est-ce que nos spé- cialistes du 10 k, comme Fiona Green et Stéphane Guertin, seront tentés par une course de grand fond ici, dans leur cour?

En prime, je m'attends presque à voir des coureurs que je n'ai pas vus depuis une mèche, ni ailleurs ni ici, Paula Ingerman, Geneviève Parent, peut-être même Steven Drinkwater?

Sur le pont Jacques Cartier, au départ, je ne vois personne que je reconnaisse. Où sont *everybody*? Je vois bien Chantale Mercier, en avant avec l'élite, et c'est tout. Est-ce la chaleur qui a rebuté les coureurs?

Courir... nulle part

Le pont Jacques Cartier donne sur l'est du centre-ville de Montréal et se verse dans le cœur des quartiers que je connais si intimement. Mais on ne fait que 100 mètres sur le pont, le temps d'une photo sous la bannière des commanditaires, et on descend aussitôt par une bretelle abrupte qui plonge dans un stationnement désert! Voilà ce que nous sommes soudain : un triste filet de coureurs sur une chaussée friable, ravagée par l'acné urbaine.

Et la chaleur qui écrase tout, et le soleil de plomb qui efface déjà tout relief... la journée va être longue!

Après les terrains déserts, et, heureusement, quelques aperçus aussi agréables que furtifs du fleuve, on s'engouffre sous les viaducs d'autoroutes aériennes et dans des recoins industriels quasiment inhabités, qui n'ont vu de vie citadine active qu'au début du siècle dernier. Luisant de sueur, la camisole détrempée, je cours seul, ou à peu près. Après la désolation du départ anonyme, je me sens comme le héros d'Alan Sillitoe: je me sens comme le dernier homme sur terre.

La vie reprend

Pour me distraire je décide de hausser la cadence. Je viens de passer la mi-course. C'est le signal de me grouiller.

C'est alors que le parcours débouche sur le boulevard de LaVérendry... et soudainement, c'est plein de gens et full animation! Des coureurs, des cyclistes, des patineurs. C'est l'anarchie, et j'adore! En entrant dans le parc Angrignon, kilomètre 28, je rattrape un coureur que je connais bien, mon ami Pierre!

- Hey Pierre!

- Salut Robert!

Presque au même moment un autre ami, Peter, se pointe à nos côtés!

- Hey Peter!

- Salut Ro-bairre!

- Peter, tu connais Pierre?

- Non, salut Pi-airre!

- Pierre, Peter!

- Salut Peter.

Nous avions l'air des trois meilleurs amis du monde, à parler de course sous la canicule.

Une autre surprise m'attendait.

- Les gars, vous voyez la petite femme, tête blanche, près du gros arbre? C'est ma mère! Je vais aller lui parler.

J'avais dit à ma mère que le marathon passerait près de chez elle. C'est la première fois qu'un membre de ma famille vient voir une compétition à laquelle je participe. La voir là me fait vraiment chaud au cœur.

Je n'ai pas voulu m'approcher trop d'elle - la sueur et l'odeur - mais je me suis installé sous son arbre. "Comment va le père, les frères, la sœur, la santé? Pas trop chaud pour être dehors?"

Je n'osais pas m'éterniser, car il me restait 14 kilomètres à courir. "Embrasse tout l'monde pour moi, je dois y aller…"

Le cœur léger, parfaitement réconcilié avec la vie, avec ce marathon et cette chaleur d'enfer, je reprends le pointillé bleu.

Je n'étais pas au bout de mes surprises.

Cent mètres plus loin, Pierre et Peter trottinent un peu en retrait du parcours, sous une lame d'ombre…

- Qu'est-ce que vous faites? Ça n'avance pas votre affaire!

- On t'attendait…

Les deux gars, qui ne se connaissaient pas il y a 10 minutes, décident de m'attendre ensemble alors que je prenais une pause pour parler avec ma mère.

Un dernier effort

Quelques kilomètres plus loin la fatigue me rattrape et pour la combattre, et espérer terminer tout d'un morceau, j'ai décidé de maintenir un bon pas, et augmenter la cadence lorsque le parcours s'y prêtait. Bref, en finir au plus sacrant!

Pierre et Peter ont opté pour une stratégie plus conservatrice qui n'aurait pas convenu à ma situation. Je ne pouvais pas me permettre d'éterniser ça. J'ai perdu Peter et Pierre alors qu'on traversait le Chinatown, en route vers le quartier latin et l'arrivée au Parc Lafontaine.

Je n'ai pas couru le marathon de Montréal depuis cette course en 2003. On me dit que le parcours est plus intéressant et l'organisation plus aguerrie d'année en année. J'y reviendrai peut-être un jour car cette course demeure marquante pour moi. Je ne suis pas prêt d'oublier ce long supplice où, pour dire comme le romancier Laurent Gaudé, la pierre gémissait de chaleur, suivi d'un moment halitueux, des plus délicieux, avec deux bons amis et ma mère au kilomètre 28... Ce que j'aimerais oublier, c'est le chrono de misère que j'ai rapporté!

Robert est un marathonien, parfois un triathlonien, et coach d'une petite équipe de marathoniennes âgées de 32 à 50 ans. Il habite et s'entraîne à Montréal. On peut le rejoindre au kilometre43@hotmail.com

Donna Davis

You will experience a first marathon only once in your life. It is best to enjoy the ride. Donna Davis from Ottawa, Ontario describes her first marathon like love at first sight.

■ *"When we got to the top there was a sign that said: "Turn around and look where you came from" - absolutely fantastic! "*

My first marathon ever - The Big Sur Marathon, Big Sur to Carmel California, was also the last day of my 39th year!

The course was spectacular and the weather was perfect, about 8 C degrees to start and 15 C at the end, overcast and no fog.

I met this amazing guy, Jay from Texas, while we were waiting in the pre-dawn hours at the start. He started running marathons at age 38 and now at 48 he is doing 100 mile ultra marathons!! He convinced me to start up near the front "Get up as close to the start line as your ego allows" he said. So there we were right behind the leaders - Yikes!

The first 10 miles were down hill from 300 ft down to 40 ft and it was hard to keep a slow pace - everyone was passing me! What was I doing up front? And of course Jay from Texas was long gone!

I met a guy from Burlington, Ontario who had flesh eating disease in his leg one year ago. His leg was saved and the Big Sur marathon was the first of 4 marathons he was running over the next month! Wow was I inspired! This helped me at mile 10, when we began the climb to hurricane point - a 2.2 mile climb around the mountains. Picture this...40 ft to 560 ft....

I had been doing the run walk (even at my slow 11 minute mile) and when I hit the hill I decided not to stop - I felt fantastic. I kept my pace and also kept reminding myself to look at the amazing scenery. I loved the hill - everyone must have been sending me good vibes because I felt really, really strong! When we got to the top there was a sign that said: "Turn around and look where you came from" - absolutely fantastic!

Running down hill to the half way point, one mile down 225 ft, I found this much harder than going up. My quads really felt the pounding, I tried to stride out but the hill was so long I couldn't keep it up, so I took some baby steps. At the bottom of the hill, was a young man playing the Grand Piano with speakers blaring out classical music. It was a surreal scene and empowering beyond belief! Thank goodness because from then on it was a whole new race. My quads were pretty tight. I told myself that they weren't so tight that I had to stop and thank God I didn't have an injury to contend with. Many were walking at this point. The last 10 miles were a mental race much more than a physical one. I was certain I could keep my pace and finish strong - mentally I was counting down the miles.

I met this young couple (his dad had done 100 marathons, this was her first and his second) and she was tired. So of course I go into coaching mode - stand up straight, drink your water, walk at the next water stop etc... "Boy" she said "How many marathons have you done?" "None" I happily said "But do I ever know how to coach!" Telling people what to do can really take your mind off your troubles.

The last hour I hooked up with Cheryl from San Francisco. This was her 5th marathon and she said it was her hardest. We were running beside each other for about a mile at the same pace so I figured we should start chatting - thank goodness we had each other. It made the last hour more bearable! She had a Garmin and was counting down the miles and the number or calories we were burning - 2500 by the end.

Just as we were coming to the finish line there was Jay from Texas wrapped in his silver blanket - he ran on to the course and gave me a big kiss on the cheek and cheered us on. I saw my husband John with a camera taking our picture. It was very touching to see how excited he was, and he kept saying he was so proud!!

Cheryl and I crossed the finish line together with lots of hugs. The sun was shining by this time and we were both pretty happy to finish. Unfortunately we lost each other in the crowd - she was definitely my angel!

That was one of the best and hardest experiences of my life; I'd do it again in a heartbeat!

Jay from Texas tracked down my email address. Here are his parting words: "To a good pal, thanks for a great time! Congratulations on your accomplishment. I must confess I never saw myself the same way after I completed my first marathon. It is a major accomplishment!"

Run strong everyone!

Donna Davis combines her love of yoga and running, and is passionate about teaching others to do the same.

www.movementtohealth.com

Chris Fretwell

Chris Fretwell

■ "The only thing keeping me going was the knowledge that I wouldn't get a shirt if I didn't finish. "

Chris Fretwell from Vancouver British Colombia tests her endurance, stomach and pain threshold during her first marathon experience. She welcomes the challenges and takes time to absorb life around her.

When I got up around 4:30 to walk the dogs, it was pouring. It was a slight 'damper' on things, but hey, this was Vancouver: what the weather was at one minute had nothing to do with what it would be the next. I added a garbage bag to my run pack and headed out the door on my great adventure.

It was beyond exciting waiting for the start. After 4 months of work we were finally there.

I followed advice and picked 3 goals for the day. The first was to finish, next to finish near 5 hours and then the lofty goal of finishing at 4:45.

I fell into my own pace and place dealing with the usual early-in-the-run shin splints. I played leap frog with an assortment of "Team in Training" and "Strides for Hope" runners during walk breaks.

Around Science World, I fell into my pace with a woman from the Bay area running for Strides for Hope. For those of you who didn't get a chance to speak to one of the 200 team members, Strides is another fundraising training team. This one is for cancer support services. There were some incredible stories.

We ran together chatting until Stanley Park and we neared the 3 hour mark. My stomach departed for places unknown and left me with some serious pain and indigestion. I told the Strides runners to go ahead. I popped some "pepcid".

It took care of a good part of the indigestion, but did nothing for the pain. I switched to a shorter run with more walk breaks. It was around then that I saw Ed out supporting us. Most of the people I've talked to mentioned running into a cheering Ed.

Around English Bay, the tummy pain increased, so did the walking, until there was no running left. By now we had been steered onto the sidewalk, to open a few roads to traffic. At one point I was running past Dee, another Strides for Hope person from Missouri, when I heard her talking to team mates on the phone. She was a bit down because she'd been alone for a while but was still going. I turned back and asked if she wanted me to walk with her. We walked for a while. She had been an early starter, so had been on the road for even longer than me. I knew I'd have to walk faster, at my own pace, or I'd never make it. So I said good bye and went off on my own. That's how I continued for the next hour or so.

I kept wanting to run, kept trying and would end up doubled over in pain. But cripes! The race would have been over sooner if I could have run more.

By the time I hit the twisty little route under the Burrard Bridge, the only thing keeping me going was the knowledge that I wouldn't get a shirt if I didn't finish. Also, combined with a very large stubborn streak - I was not quitting!! And of course, the wonderful sun came out! Even if I hadn't forgotten my sun block, it wouldn't have been effective 5 hours later, so along with the expected leg, hip, back stiffness, I got a lovely lobster shade anywhere that wasn't covered by clothes.

On the bridge, at the 40K, I hit the emotional roller coaster. Anytime anyone offered encouragement, I started crying. I had an interesting time convincing the bike guides that I was really okay. I tried running again. The lump in my stomach had been joined by a lump in my throat. I finally got it all under control, or maybe I just didn't care about pain anymore. I ran most of the way back along Pacific. I could hear the announcer as I approached the finish line. If it hadn't been a cute little kid on a chair putting the metals around necks, I would have just grabbed mine because my stomach tried one final huge lurch. I crossed at 6:48:36, a couple of hours slower than I hoped, but a finish none the less.

Sounds like an adventure eh, but I really only have 1 question....."When's the next one!!!" Yes, I'm hooked! Insane but hooked! I want to do another marathon! I want to run one with the regular walk breaks, and no more!

Congrats to all my friends who also met the challenge head on. We are all winners!

Chris Fretwell teaches running clinics in Vancouver, and claims she has a soft spot for the Running Room for getting her where she is today. She has completed 2 marathons and has raised funds for the Arthritis Society. "I'm not a fast runner, but I'm a determined one with a love for the sport." She wants to buy several copies of this book as she thinks they would make nice gifts!

Rosaire Gagné

Rosaire Gagné

■ *"Ajouter des marathons aux marathons, c'est un dépassement, un défi humain qui met de la vie dans mes années. "*

Rosaire Gagné, marathonien de Montréal, Québec nous inspire avec une capacité de rêver au-delà des nuages. En 2006, il a couru son 100ième marathon dans sa ville, Montréal. Il a joué le rôle de "meneur d'allure" pour aider d'autres coureurs à réaliser leur rêve. Il ajoute que son objectif ultime est de vivre jusqu'à 100 ans....en santé.

Quand on me demande: "Pourquoi courir tant de marathons?" Je réponds: "Pour le défi". En fait, toute la vie est un défi à chaque jour. Pour certains, le simple fait de vivre ou même de se lever quotidiennement est un défi selon la condition physique de chaque être humain. Vivre est un défi, un dépassement, un aller plus loin, plus haut, plus vite. Vivre, c'est ajouter des jours, des mois et des années à sa vie. Qui ne désire pas "un plus" dans sa vie? Quand on se regarde vivre, on constate qu'on en veut toujours plus... Se dépasser, dans quelque domaine que ce soit, c'est humain. Comme on dit: "C'est la vie!"

Courir un marathon, c'est un défi; en courir plusieurs, c'est un autre "plus". Car, on le sait, le marathon, c'est une distance au-delà des limites de l'humain comme l'Everest est au-delà des limites de la montagne. Voilà pourquoi, montagnes après montagnes, l'alpiniste veut atteindre ce sommet. Le marathon demeure une distance mythique pour un coureur, comme l'Everest l'est pour l'alpiniste. Je me dis parfois que si j'avais découvert l'alpinisme, j'aurais certainement voulu gravir l'Everest!

Est-ce bon pour la santé? Courir, c'est l'exercice qui met le plus en forme, pas de doute là-dessus. Courir beaucoup... vers un centième marathon? Je crois aussi que la santé y gagne, à condition de le faire avec modération en oubliant la performance. Le marathon demeure toujours une épreuve physique difficile même si pour moi, l'appréhension du débutant est disparue. Après chaque marathon, je termine "crevé"! C'est normal. Mais, je récupère rapidement. N'est-ce pas cela la bonne forme?

Ajouter des marathons aux marathons, c'est un dépassement, un défi humain qui met de la vie dans mes années. Je m'y suis laissé prendre et, le plaisir croissant avec l'usage, je m'achemine bientôt vers un centième. Cent, devient un chiffre mythique comme le marathon lui-même. Je connais plusieurs marathoniens qui ont dépassé de beaucoup cet objectif. Serait-ce que pour eux le défi continue, la vie continue... "Faut pas lâcher", quelque soit son défi.

Rosaire, est âgé de 66 ans, et retraité de l'enseignement. Il pratique la course à pied depuis une trentaine d'années. En 1979, lors du premier marathon de Montréal, il commence son aventure de marathonien qui le mène à travers le Canada, les États-Unis et l'Europe. Ayant déjà participé à des ultra marathons (12 heures et 100 km) il m'assure que les distances ne lui font pas peur.

Scott Haldane

This story from Toronto, Ontario gives an account as a spectator at the Boston Marathon. It is a memorable and inspiring story which is stranger than fiction. It is about some of the interesting things that happen to people involved with running. It acknowledges that a runner's community is at the heart of the marathon experience.

■ *"When does a coincidence become so much more than chance?"*

Sometimes in life, things happen that were meant to be. They resist rational explanation. Friendships can now have an even more special dimension....one that neither of us can explain. We can only accept and be grateful.

I would like to tell you my story.

My wife was running her second Boston Marathon and I was there to cheer her on. I decided to take the subway to Boston College and wait at the 21 mile mark at the top of Heartbreak Hill.

None of us had counted on the heat: 87 degrees – the second hottest Boston on record! I knew it was going to be a tough day for all runners. The elite women and men seemed to be way off their projected times and the runners were all in obvious discomfort when they reached the top of Heartbreak Hill.

As the runners began to pass in greater numbers, I saw the first person that I recognized, Dave McConkey. Dave is normally a 2:50 marathoner, but he was on a 3:45 pace. I jumped into the stream of runners and began to run alongside Dave. "How's it going?" I asked. "It's brutal. I've backed off my time and I'm just trying to finish." he replied."Well, hang in there." I encouraged him. I peeled away from Dave a hundred yards or so down the road. As I turned to head back to the 21 mile mark, I caught sight of someone out of the corner of my eye who I thought I recognized.

"Ralph?" I called. It was Ralph Westgarth. I had met Ralph years ago in the 1990 Montreal Marathon. I helped Ralph achieve his 3:10 goal and we've been friends ever since. We meet frequently at races and have kept track of each other's running career. And now.....here was Ralph!! I jumped into the race beside Ralph, but he was quick to tell me his calf was locked, he was all cramped up, and could I massage his calf. I looked down at his calf and it looked like a baseball.

I saw an empty chair and I told Ralph to sit down as I tried to release the cramp in his calf. While I was working on it without success (based on Ralph's screams), a stranger came along and began giving Ralph instructions to pull his toes towards his knee and then to push them down. He seemed to know what he was doing and Ralph said that the cramp was easing up. I asked how he knew what to do and he said that he was a massage therapist. "You're in luck Ralph!" I said "This guy knows what he's doing."

Just as I said this, Ralph screamed, "My other leg is cramping!" It seemed like a jolt of electricity coursed through Ralph's body from his right foot up his right leg and into his chest and shoulders. He stiffened like a board and stopped screaming completely. I looked at his face and he was grey....all the colour had disappeared. "He's in serious trouble!" I yelled "Can you get medical attention?" I asked the massage therapist who ran off to find help. Ralph's cheeks were all sucked in and I removed his sunglasses to see his eyes. I'll never forget how they looked! His eyes were open and staring. There was no pupil dilation.

Someone in the crowd shouted: "He's not breathing!"

I could also see that he was not breathing. I tried to find a pulse on his neck, but could feel nothing. We lifted him off the chair and onto the ground. I had been a lifeguard 30 years ago and knew instantly that I had to give Ralph CPR! Someone from the crowd began to give him chest compressions as I tilted

Ralph's head, pinched his nostrils and gave him mouth-to-mouth. I gave him three breaths and Ralph began to sputter! I was terribly relieved to see him come back!!

It was incredible! In what seemed like less than a minute, Ralph said, "I'm feeling much better now!" and then, "I think I can run!" I said "I think you're done for the day Ralph, the medics are on their way". Ralph insisted on running, but agreed to let them check him out.

When the medics arrived with a gurney stretcher, I pulled one of them aside and told him what had happened. I knew that Ralph might try to talk them into letting him run if I didn't give them the whole story. At the medical tent, they put Ralph on an IV. His blood pressure was 80/40. They let him recover for half an hour. At the end of this time he was feeling much better and asked if he could re-enter. The world started spinning when he tried to stand up, and even Ralph agreed that he was, indeed, out of the race.

Ralph and I are now left with so many questions. When does a coincidence become so much more than chance? Ralph and I had met 14 years ago at the Montreal marathon. We had paced each other to complete our goal of a 3:10 finish. Over the years, we've met by accident more often than by plan. Why did I choose to be a marathon spectator rather than a participant? Why did I choose the 21-mile mark to peel away from my friend Dave McConkey? How did I spot and recognize Ralph out of the corner of my eye? How can it be that when I had to give CPR to one of the 18,000 runners who participated that day, the person who collapsed at my feet was a friend I had known for almost 15 years?!

For Ralph and me, our friendship will now have an even more special dimension....one that neither of us can explain.....we can only accept and be grateful.

Scott Haldane is President of YMCA greater Toronto, husband, father and has run 19 marathons.

It proved to me, and hopefully to others that anything is possible. It has taught
challenging, my head down and I'm there. The timing feels right
you don't even know screaming your name and cheering you on! Me they w
marathon runner. Conquering that challenge was awesome, and to know all th
to others that anything is possible. It has taught me that you can find strength
head down and I'm there. The timing feels right for me to embark on fulfilling
your name and cheering you on! Me, they were talking about me, a marathon
challenge was awesome, and to know all that I had to overcome to get there n

t you can find strength in the deepest places. As the banner gets closer, I see a
to embark on fulfilling this 42.2K dream. Oh, what it felt like to have people
king, a marathoner! A strong father, husband, cancer survivor and
d to overcome to get there made it even better. It proved to me, and hopefully
eepest places. As the banner gets closer, I see a digital clock ticking out my
2K dream. Oh, what it felt like... don't even know screaming
rong father, husband, cancer survivor... a run runner...
even better. It proved to me, and hopefully to others that anything is possible.

Proved *strength* *survivor* *POSSIBLE*

■ He that can't
endure the bad will
not live to see the
good.

~ *Yiddish proverb*

Jennifer Henry

■ *"More draining than the physical challenge, fears and apprehensions work in concert to drain your energy."*

Jennifer Henry from North Tetagouche, New Brunswick raises money, awareness and is changed forever. Get the Kleenex, you might need it.

Inspired by my friend's decision to get involved with The Arthritis Society's Joints In Motion (JIM) program, I decided to start my thirties in a significant manner. I signed up for the JIM marathon two days before my 30th birthday.

My marathon is in Flanders Fields, Ypres, Belgium. Try as I might to focus on enjoying myself that day, I was plagued with doubts, apprehensions and tons of nervousness.

The race starts!

About an hour into the race, I felt a nagging tightness behind my knee. I would always steal moments of time to stretch during our walk intervals.

My knee pain was becoming more bothersome and I was beginning to wonder how this would play itself out over the next 30 kilometres. I expressed my concerns to my running mates and they suggested that I slow down and stretch more.

The reality of what I was doing was dawning on me. I was in the middle of a marathon! What on earth was I doing here? The nearer the three-hour mark got, the stronger my fear grew. All of my training had taught me that a marathon is two percent physical and ninety-eight percent mental. More draining than the physical challenge, fears and apprehensions work in concert to drain your energy.

The wise words of my trainers were screaming in my head: "Do nothing on marathon day that you have not tried during your training." My instincts, however, were telling me that I needed food. It was at about this time that we met up with our trainer Daryl Steeves.

Equipped with a bike, medical supplies, food and encouragement, Daryl descended upon me as an angel descends from the heavens. His smiling face and words of comfort lifted me in ways I couldn't even begin to describe. By then, my knee was creating a serious impact on my running.

Completing this journey would now require a deliberate effort to put one foot in front of the other. Alas, the pain in my knee and my growing disappointment of not finishing within my five and a half hour goal were wearing me down. I was truly alone with my pain, my doubts and my fears.

Daryl mended my knee, offered a few kind words of caution and encouragement and he was off. Watching him ride away was the single most excruciating thing I had experienced that day. I wept until I thought my heart would break.

I was desperately grasping for any frayed string left from my training to no avail. I has hitting the wall, and hitting it hard.

Then, through my tear-blurred vision I beheld a strange sight: a JIM participant running in the wrong direction!

To this day, I cannot explain how or why he showed up when he did, but this JIM trainer from Calgary was my saving grace. He asked how I was feeling and listened quietly as I poured out my sweaty and pain-ridden soul.

He helped me get my mind off my pain. He made me slow down and walk without my really noticing. And, he gave me an opportunity to reflect on the true reasons why I decided to run this marathon. From that moment on, I knew that things would be okay.

I had more clarity of purpose at that moment than I had ever felt.

I thought of my mom, my arthritis hero, and the pain that she lives with every single day of her life. I thought of all the funds raised by our team in the hopes of improving the lives of those who suffer from arthritis.

I thought of the temporary nature of my own pain and how incredibly lucky I was to even be here.

I felt the loving embrace of my mother's spirit lift me and carry me those last six K to the finish. I wept because I knew that I was already victorious, because my one small act had impacted not only my life forever, but also the lives of the ones I love and will touch the lives of those who will benefit from the Arthritis Society's work. I wept because I was on the verge of completing one of the hardest tasks I had ever given myself.

I decided to put my pain aside and run the remaining 800 meters.

I smiled despite the pain and kept on smiling as I saw the enormous clock that had witnessed every marathoner's finish, heard the cheers from the crowd and crossed the finish line. And then I cried. Not the proud and dignified tears one sheds when she has accomplished something wonderful, but full-blown sobbing with tears heavily rolling off my face that spoke to the overwhelming sense of pride, accomplishment, emotion and pure pain I felt but could not vocalize. It swept me into an emotional tailspin that still sways me to this day.

We remained until the very end, watching the last JIM participant cross the finish line, huge Canadian flag in tow. We lingered on afterwards, taking pictures, sharing in each others' journeys of victory and basking in our newfound titles as marathoners.

This experience has shaped me in innumerable ways. It continues to influence my outlook on all things important. It has taught me that you will find strength in the deepest places when something is really worth doing; that every journey begins with that first step; and that you must take things one step at a time.

Jennifer is a mother and co-producer, with her husband, of a television series "Fishing Musicians". She also manages the New Brunswick Association of Community Business Development Corporations. She no longer runs, yet she is seriously contemplating participating in another JIM marathon for her 40th birthday.

Photo courtesy of Phil Marsh

Noel Hulsman

■ *"Now every so often my arms seem to go numb and I occasionally feel a shiver up my spine. Are those the beginning signs of heatstroke?"*

Noel Hulsman, from Vancouver BC immediately inspired me with his account of the LA Marathon. Water, crowds, mental games, yes, truly man's best friend.

It's not yet 8 a.m. and the temperature has pushed past 75 F, almost 20 degrees above the norm. I'm at the intersection of Figueroa and Fifth Street in downtown Los Angeles. In just over half-an-hour, a gun will fire, signaling the start of the 19th L.A. Marathon.

On the podium, a block away, there's a discernible edge in the race marshal's voice. "It is going to be hot today," he repeats again and again into the mike, "do not run past the water stations." Unsaid is "or else", but you know he's thinking it. He's about to send 24,532 runners into one of the hottest March 7ths in L.A. history. There's no shade on the course and 95 per cent of the runners will still be slogging it out well past noon. I'm praying I won't be one of them.

Having run three (out of four) Vancouver marathons in unrelenting downpours, this year I resolved to find a race where there would be almost no chance of rain. True to my usual attention to detail, I picked one that falls right on the shoulders of Southern Cal's rainy season, but I didn't realize that, and anyway, the allure of running through an L.A. empty of traffic was too tantalizing to pass up.

The route is a 26.2 mile version of

the American dream. Drawn together below the towers of commerce downtown, we'll run towards the mean streets of South-Central before working our way west into blue-collar Latino turf. From there we'll advance through 'moving-on-up' Sikh and Jewish neighborhoods before arriving on the landscaped lawns of Beverly Hills. Then it's back downtown, prouder and richer for having pursued the journey. Or, at least that's my thinking before the marathon starts, when it's all still theoretical. And then the gun goes off. The first half-mile is all knees and elbows, a flock of flamingos scrambling past each other to get ahead. My aim is to finish in three-and-a-half hours, which means averaging eight-minute miles. To help, I've saddled up behind 'Jay', the designated 3:30 pace group leader. But when he bolts from the starting line, it's clear he's either going way too fast, or I've got to speed up.

We're barely one mile in, and already I'm forsaking the first immutable law of marathon running: don't push too hard, too soon. The first mile takes us south past the Staples Center, home of the NBA Lakers and the L.A. Kings, and then over to the L.A. Coliseum, the 94,159-seat stadium that hosted much of the '84 Olympics. I'm struggling too hard to stay close to Jay but to my left there seems to be a DC-8 parked on the University of Southern California campus. I can't tell why.

Turning onto Martin Luther King Blvd. we enter a strip of cinder-block apartments with bars on the windows. This is Boyz in the Hood turf. African-American gospel choirs shout hallelujahs from sidewalks, and families gather on the balconies and stoops, staring at us in what looks like befuddled amusement.

By Mile 7, my pace group has petered out into a single file, the slowest runners dropping off one by one. I need to pee, but if I pull over, Jay will be gone.

At Mile 10 we turn on to Venice Blvd. In the distance I can see the Hollywood Hills and Century City. This is a celebrity-mad city, though as far as I can tell, there are no stars in the race.

Near the halfway mark, the crowds are starting to build. We're now at La Cienaga a neighborhood of Catholic churches. In truth, that could be all of L.A. Forty-five per cent of the population is Latino, a fact reflected in the billboards, restaurants and all of the public signs.

Mile 16 lands in Little Ethiopia, home of Mo Better Meaty Meat Burgers and the Black Dahlia Theatre. I can still see Jay, but he's shrinking in the distance. Not that it matters, but the race is probably officially over by now. Last year's winner, Kenyan Mark Yatich wrapped it up in 2:09:52, (though still falling well short of Simon Bor's 2:04:55 world mark). To speed up the process this year, race organizers are staging 'battle of the sexes', offering an extra US$50,000 to the first runner across the finish line, and then giving the elite women a 20-minute head start.

Miles 17 to 19 are always the loneliest. The adrenalin has worn thin, your dogs are barking, yet the finish line is a distant dream. Fortunately, we're now heading towards Beverly Hills, a neighborhood that'll surely have some palm trees for shade. In the more heavily Latino areas, residents were out with their hoses and sprinklers, kindly dousing us as we ran past. But I fear the Beverly Hills set won't be as familiar with their gardening gear.

To keep up with Jay, I've succeeded in peeing twice without breaking stride but at the 20-mile mark, it's no use, he's gone. Now every so often my arms seem to go numb and I occasionally feel a shiver up my spine. Are those the beginning signs of heat stroke? Maybe, because along the road the number of runners being attended to by medics appears to have grown exponentially. (Almost 5,000 people will end up dropping out).

Every year, officials in L.A. are criticized over the race's relatively late 8:30 a.m. start yet that aside, their level of organization can't be faulted. In addition to the choirs and cheerleading squads, there are some 12,000 volunteers serving up water, Gatorade, gels, oranges and other goodies along the course.

By Mile 23 I'm nearing Koreatown, but if there's anything interesting to see it's lost on me. My head is down and I'm wondering whether puking is also something you can do on the fly. With Jay gone, I'm no longer sure of my pace, only that it's slower. My stopwatch reads 3:08, which means a decent time is within reach, but sadly, not a 3:30.

The final three miles are a blur of emotions and pain. I'm not worried anymore about heat stroke or cramping up. I'm thinking about those countless long runs on soaking wet mornings in the winter. This is the payoff, right now.

At Mile 25 I'm almost back amidst the skyscrapers. Crossing Figueroa, I see runners turning north around the next bend. Surely that has to be the last corner. When I reach it, I see in the distance a thin yellow banner. And now the crowd is huge, lined five deep on the sidewalk. As the banner gets closer, I can see a digital clock ticking 3:36:17, 18, 19. I put my head down and I'm there.

Noel Hulsman is now living in Toronto and works as an editor with the Globe&Mail.

Lorraine Johannson

■ *"Training, with all other responsibilities, is a challenge of balance."*

Lorraine Johannson, from Calgary, Alberta gave herself the best gift for her 40th birthday. She shares her gift with all of us. Thank you for the inspiration.

One day while skating with my son at the Olympic Oval in Calgary, I began watching the runners on the running track. I had participated in long distance running in the past and I felt this soulful call to get back on the right track.

Running takes me to a place that is so calming and inspirational.

The emotional momentum was the biggest factor in my journey. I have been the single parent of a son who has changed my world. Parenting and a full time job have taken my time and energy over the years but as my son grows older the timing feels right for me to embark on fulfilling this 42.2 K dream.

I am going to run a marathon for my 40th birthday. This will be my gift to me. I have chosen to run the Royal Victoria Marathon in Victoria, British Columbia.

To help me train, I joined a running club. It got me through the intensely difficult moments and I loved celebrating all the personal bests: best time, longest distance, no pain, healed injuries. It was never easy, but always acowledged for either my strong 34K run or my very tired and difficult 6K run. It was always a celebration of stretching, coffee, warm clothing, hugs, smiles and tears.

My focus was to cross the finish line healthy and smiling. It was one step at a time from beginning to end. For me it was a challenge to balance my training with all of my other responsibilities.

I had to make one of the most difficult decisions by leaving my son in Calgary with his Grandma while I traveled to the start line. I needed to be clear and focused on what I was about to accomplish, and I could share this experience with him when I returned.

It was time to pack my bags. I was offered this advice: "Do not put your running clothes and especially your shoes in your suitcase. Carry those items with you at all times during your travel". Good advice. How distressing it would have been to arrive without the shoes I had been training in. It is a law of running to do nothing new come race day.

Marathon morning was cool and refreshing. I was grateful for having chosen such a beautiful location. Heather, who had kept me company so many times on our training runs, would run along side me today.

I was determined to settle into a pace, listen, chat and make sure that Heather and I took our breaks. We had trained with a schedule to run 10 minutes and then walk for one minute. This method of long distance running helps to keep up a runner's energy throughout the race. 5 hours later I was thankful for those one minute moments.

Here are all the other things that I was grateful for along the way. The ocean views were breathtaking. The fresh air was inspirational. The encouragement of the volunteers and fans along the route brought a smile even when it was difficult. I loved the music that brought a rhythm to each step until my pace fell off.

The last 6K of the race was difficult, rewarding and exciting. Difficult because of exhaustion, rewarding because I was going to finish and exciting because I was focused on reaching the top of a long hill! There was a house at the top of that hill that had been in my line of vision and I saw nothing else. But I did hear my name! It was my friend Valentine, who was also running and sharing this difficult, last stretch.

The last few moments felt like real life in slow motion. I had been running for 5 hours and I did not want to finish. The people were cheering, and photos were being taken! One more smile and it was over! I had crossed the finish line of a marathon!

I could now celebrate this gift of courage, strength, perseverance and love.

Lorraine has recently run a 21.1K race with her son. Her next one will be her 10th! She plans to run a third marathon soon! "I have learned that life is about passion. Find your passion and you have found life. I feel that a commitment to our own happiness makes the world a better place for us all." Lorraine's son has just completed his first marathon and finished 2nd in his age category.

Annie Koppens

Annie Koppens

■ "Wonder Woman, I couldn't have done it without you - I owe my finish to you." Wow".

If you can't have fun at a marathon, something is missing. Annie Koppens, from Pembroke, Ontario offers up plenty of lessons that remind marathon runners to have fun. Take notes!

Standing in Corral 12 that morning, with a stomach full of butterflies and a smile so big it seemed to bounce off of those around her, was a very enthusiastic girl ready to run her second-ever marathon. Surrounded by hundreds of other nervous, excited runners my age, I wouldn't have been nearly so noticeable had I not also been wearing the costume of my childhood hero, Wonder Woman.

On a poster given out to all participants, Adidas summed up the Boston marathon as "Everything you ever needed to know about yourself you will learn in 26.2 miles."

Crossing the finish line 4 hours and 24 minutes later, my costume was no longer simply a disguise, but the perfect outfit for how I was feeling; I had completed the Boston marathon, and I was a true wonder woman.

This is my story.

Prancing around in my Wonder Woman costume I found myself to be right in the centre of attention!

I must have had my photo taken with 200 or so other runners. As soon as the warm up clothes came off, people swarmed me. I had my photo taken for the Boston Globe, and was even interviewed by Boston's Channel 4 news! I told the world (well, all of Boston) that I come from Deep River, Ontario and when asked how one trains for a marathon during the winter, I said "Ya suck it up!"

The first 15K was all up and down, the spectators lined 10-15 people thick every inch of the road. Runners slowly found their pace and began to thin out. My first 15K were fast and strong - unfortunately, more than a bit too fast. It was 25 C; the heat was quite a shock to my system, having just come from a place where there was still snow on the ground! It was unexpected, and I was unprepared.

I did not take a step without someone yelling "Go Wonder Woman!" I was laughing my head off, having the time of my life, high-fiving everybody, moving with power. I wasn't even thinking of the running, I was so caught up in the spectators and people loving my costume.

Just before 20K, I knew I was in trouble. My head was spinning and my stomach was churning. I was going too fast and the sun and excitement were overwhelming me. I honestly thought I would drop, and along came an angel - he asked how I was doing. I told him I couldn't hang on. He told me I had to slow down. Slowing down has never been an option for me - everything I do, I do with passion and speed - but I also finish everything I do, and I knew if I kept up that crazy pace, I wasn't going to finish this race.

He went on ahead and I told my legs to slow down. Immediately I felt the smile return to my face, my body begin to relax, and my legs return to their comfort zone.

I wish I had had a tape recorder; I wish you could hear how they cheered for me! And not just for Wonder Woman - I had taped "ANNIE" to my back, so they were screaming my name too! Oh, what it felt like to have thousands of people you don't even know screaming your name and cheering you on! WOW!! WOW!! WOW!!!

Now begins the hard part - you're over halfway there, but your body just wants to give up. This is when it is your mind that does most of the work, forcing your legs to keep moving.

I also did some encouraging as well - at one point I put my arm around a guy who was walking and said "C'mon buddy, let's go - I want to see you at the finish - you can do it!"

This guy actually found me at the end in a crowd of thousands of other runners and their families and gave me a huge, sweaty hug, and said "Wonder Woman, I couldn't have done it without you - I owe my finish to you". Wow.

By Mile 22 my legs had turned to logs. I was in the worst condition I have ever been in, in all of the races I've ever run. The heat, my too-energetic start, lack of food and the overwhelming excitement were really weighing down on me. I looked into the crowds as they swam past me and tried to find a face, just one face, to hold onto for strength.

I will never forget the people who cheered for me; the kids holding out their hands for high-fives, the adults clapping, the students yelling, everyone encouraging you to keep going, keep going. It was just incredible.

At mile 25 I was in Boston, and with the end in site, I found new strength. My last two miles were strong, my arms rose in the air, tears streaming, mouth grinning.

The last ½ mile stretch had spectators packed 30 or so people thick. Their cheering became a dull roar as the voice inside my own head took over, saying "You did it, baby, you did it!!!"

I came in strong, proud, and jubilant, blowing a kiss directly into the face of a camera staring me down. I had lived, loved, and revelled in every single one of those minutes.

And now I, Annie, am a Boston Marathoner.

Annie Koppens, wife, teacher, and new mom, lives in Pembroke, Ontario. She has run a total of three marathons, and has recently begun doing triathlons. A picture of Annie dressed as Wonder Woman at the Boston Marathon hangs in her classroom. She never tires of sharing her story with her students and encouraging them to go for their dreams, and to never give up.

Photo courtesy of Chris Laundry

Bruno Lacroix

■ *"The runners around me must have thought I was losing it when I started talking out loud to my kids, "Come on guys, bring daddy in, you can do it".*

Athletes are taught to use imagery. Bruno Lacroix from Gatineau, Quebec shows us the power of imagery to make it thru his marathon. No doubt his children have angel wings.

I remember when I first started running 11 months ago and how I could only run 2.5 kms at the time, with walk breaks.

Here I am the night before my first marathon, thinking of the distance I'm going to run tomorrow morning. 42.2K! Wow that's a long way!

An enthusiastic friend had nagged me for three weeks to try running before I finally did.

Today I thank him.

My friend and I were both registered for the Montreal Marathon in September, but I was so anxious to run a marathon that I convinced him to run the Quebec City marathon at the end of August.

Somehow running two marathons within two weeks of each other seemed like a good idea.

Morning comes and we're boarding the buses, which will bring us to the Start line. It's a hazy day, 18 Celsius and they are forecasting rain. The bus ride takes so long to drive the Marathon route that I'm tempted to ask the driver if he's lost. I'm really going to run all this distance! The thought is as scary as it is exciting.

The gun goes off and we start running through the streets of Levis, a suburb of Quebec City. We wind our way through the residential neighbourhoods with the residents cheering us on. My buddy and I decided to each run at our own pace, so we wish each other luck and he takes off.

Ten minutes later the rain comes. It's not a bit of rain that is going to prevent me from prevailing today!

I tap a few kids' hands and before I know it 10 kms go by. Although I'm feeling good, my Garmin is telling me that my pace is way too fast. I feel I'm going at a good pace but if I go too fast I might bonk out and hit the wall (which I have eluded so far in my running life). I push aside my worries and continue at the same pace. If I can make it to the bridge into Quebec City then I should be fine.

We continue running along the Saint-Lawrence seaway shoreline with a superb view of Quebec City. Everything is going well and my hill training is paying off on the steep hills. It's still raining so there aren't a lot of spectators, but they are very energetic!

A group of school-age kids are all sitting together and they scream really loud as the runners pass by. I don't know if they realize it, but they'll be etched in my mind forever. They gave me so much energy when I passed them.

I keep looking for the bridge but I can't see it yet. The rain hasn't let up and I'm soaking wet from head to toe. Each step I take feels squishy in my shoes. I start second guessing my decision to keep the same pace and I need something to give me a boost.

So far I haven't put on my mp3 player. I wanted to save it for the last 13 kms after the bridge, but I can't see the bridge! A few hills later I finally spot it and a sigh of relief comes with it. I keep telling myself to wait for the other side before putting on my mp3 player.

Immediately on the other side I start listening to music. It's all in my head, a few good tunes, a downhill and a power gel are exactly what I need after running 32 kms. They say the real race starts with 10 K to go. Now I feel ready to take it on!

At 34 kms I start worrying about the wall, but tell myself to quit it and keep up the pace.

At 36 kms I'm getting really tired, so I start imagining I'm back home running with my kids on each side of me on their bikes. The runners around me must have thought I was losing it when I started talking out loud to my kids, "Come on guys, bring daddy in, you can do it".

I spot what looks like my friend up ahead. Catching up to him has become my sole point of focus. Two kilometres later I finally do. As we turn the corner into the final 300 meter stretch, I turn to my friend and ask him if he wants to sprint to the end. The look on his face said it all, but he still muttered out "No, you go".

With 200 meters left, I took off and ran as fast as my legs would take me.

As I'm crossing the finish line I look up at the clock and see 3:41:45.What a beautiful sight!!

All of a sudden my legs are so cramped, I cannot walk. How was it that just 5 minutes ago I was running and now I look like a constipated penguin? Although they're too young to understand, I tell my kids about what I accomplished and I thank them for being with me on my journey.

Bruno is a software designer who says he was NEVER athletic. He has run 3 marathons and holds a PB of 3:17. He is married and a father of two children. He also likes to play a Chinese game called GO....

Photo courtesy of Carl Wagar

■ Don't look back,
unless you plan to
go that way.
~ *Anonymous*

Shannon Loutitt

■ *"For every negative thought that crept into my mind, a picture of Tom would appear, along with the feelings of strength, courage and incredible determination. "*

Shannon, from Saskatoon Saskatchewan became my inspiration to continue with my vision of publishing a book of Canadian marathon stories. This story parallels life. It describes where we come from, what we are capable of, and what lies ahead.

Stories like Tom Longboat's need to be shared and remembered by everyone. Without hearing the story the messages would be lost. These stories not only inspire, but have the power to completely change the direction of a person's life. I know, because it happened to me!

Before the Tom Longboat story, there is the story of my great-grandfather Billy Loutitt.

During the river break-up in the spring of 1904, the small town of Athabasca, Alberta, became captive to a great flood from a nearby river and needed immediate emergency assistance from the city of Edmonton. The Hudson Bay Company stood to lose a great deal from the flood. Two messengers were dispatched to get help. One messenger was sent on horseback, from Stony Creek, 80 miles north of Edmonton. The other messenger was sent on foot, from Athabasca 100 miles north of Edmonton. This messenger, a Metis dispatch carrier, was my great-grandfather. My great-grandfather ran cross-country through flooded terrain, and made it to Edmonton in 16 hours, an hour before the guy on horseback! We were told that in honour of my grandfather's heroics, the town of

Athabasca hosts an annual Triathlon in his name, called 'The Billy Loutitt Dispatch Triathlon'.

Later, I asked my husband, "What is a triathlon?"

The lives of my family members and I changed forever. We were now embarking on a new direction. The following year I competed in 6 Triathlons, including "The Billy Loutitt" in Athabasca, and "The World Masters Championships" in Edmonton. I had age-group placements in all, except one. I had also completed my first half-marathon. Damian, my then 6 yr old, competed in 4 triathlons in 2005, and was the first of his generation to complete his great-great-grandfather's race. All this from one story!

One would think that this type of life changing inspiration, comes to a person but once in their lifetime. Not so! Shortly after my 2nd season of triathlon, I was told the story of Tom Longboat.

I was so amazed at how this aboriginal man became "The Man Who Ran Faster than Everyone". Amidst much skepticism and racial challenges, he set the world-record during the 1907 Boston Marathon, beating the previous record by 5 minutes.

Inspired by Longboat I decided to try to qualify and run the 2007 Boston marathon in his honour. In January 2006, I set out on my journey for Boston. With my running book 'Running - Start to Finish' by John Stanton, I trained hard. Through much sweat and tears, I got myself to my first marathon in Regina, Saskatchewan, on September 10th, 2006. I finished a disappointing 6 minutes away from qualifying for Boston. I signed up for the Toronto marathon scheduled four weeks after Regina. Everything rode on this Toronto marathon. I needed to finish in 3 hrs and 40 minutes or I would lose my opportunity to commemorate our national hero, Tom Longboat.

I started out the race at a faster than normal pace and was feeling the backlash of such a pace at the 15km mark. My breathing was laboured and I could feel the cramps around my stomach coming on, so I tossed my bottles of water and opted for the aid stations instead of the extra weight. My eyes and legs stayed steady with the 3:30 pace bunny, and I prayed that I could maintain this rate for another 27km. With so far to go, and the pace bunny slowly disappearing in the distance, my thoughts and feelings were not very positive. My husband, bless his soul, gave his best rendition of a Saskatchewan Prairie Dog, and was popping up at every other aid station to cheer me on. The wonderful people of Toronto also did their part to try and motivate me further down the road by hollering "Go Shannon Go!" As my body started to waver and spirits started to falter, one thought kept my legs moving and propelled me forward towards the finish - Tom Longboat. For every negative thought that crept into my mind, a picture of Tom would appear, along with feelings of strength, courage and incredible determination. I would imagine him running with me, along with my great-grandfather, and say to myself, "just this once, just this once, then it's Boston".

As I closed in on the finish line, a wave of anticipation engulfed me, and with the spirits of these grandfathers running with me, I broke out into a sprint. Running faster and faster for the last 200 meters, I crossed the finish line at an incredible 3 hours and 35 minutes! Eleven minutes quicker than four weeks prior! Thank you so much grandfathers, thank you so much Tom!

So here again, two amazing stories have set my family on another incredible journey. Thank you Tom Longboat & Billy Loutitt for all that you have given! See you in Boston!

Shannon Loutitt attributes her successes to her partner and her 7yr old son. She has a background in business. She is renovating her 1929 home when not running.

Photo courtesy of Phil Marsh

■ "He who
hesitates is not
only lost, but
miles from the
next exit"
~ *Unknown*

Arthur Munro

Arthur Munro, from Aylmer, Quebec, teaches a lesson in courage. I don't know that I could have done what Arthur had to do on race day.

■ *"Now how many first time marathoners get a police escort for the first 10K!?"*

A friend of mine, who had run a marathon inspired me to purchase John Stanton's book, "Start to Finish". I followed the training schedule for a 3:30 marathon race but really had aspirations of qualifying for Boston. My friends think I have a Type-A personality. I guess this just reinforces that notion.

Many people tell me how stressful the start line can be so I had a great plan. Hang out at Tim Horton's until nearly the start, then make my way and go for it!

I ask a race official where the start line is. "Start line for what?" he replies. "The marathon of course" I stutter out, a bit perplexed about why he does not know where the start line is. "The marathon is gone, they left at 7 am." My heart momentarily stopped beating. I gathered my composure and said "Are you sure?" His expression changed from being helpful to completely perplexed. "Absolutely!" he replies. "Oh shit!" was all that would come out of my mouth! What should I do now? Go home? Sit down and cry?

I made a brave decision to go for it regardless! I took off my sweats, checked my bag as fast as I could, sprinted to the start line, queued my watch and took off like a mad man!

By this time traffic had resumed on the road and I was forced to run on the side walk. Over the bridge I ran, or should I say sprinted! I rounded the corner and began to settle into a pace. As I ran by race officials at each bend and curve, the completely puzzled looks soon turned to encouraging cheering as they shouted "Go get 'em", or "Nice pace, you can do it". All was going fine until I rounded the corner and saw all the runners returning back to the other side. Back up on the side walk for me! Running

through water stations, all race volunteers were facing the returning runners and not my direction. I had to help myself to the liquids.

As I rounded the corner across the bridge to the Rockcliffe Parkway area, I was joined by the nicest medic on a bicycle. The first thing she asked was "Did you take a break or something?". Now remembering that I started an hour late, this made me chuckle very hard. What kind of person runs a marathon with an hour break right at the beginning!? She informs me that she will ride with me until I catch the tail end runners. I guess she had confidence that I would catch them due to the fact I was running like a wolf in heat.

Eventually we were joined by a police officer on a motorcycle who took up the vigilance. Now how many first time marathoners get a police escort for the first 10 kms?

I passed my first Marathon Runner about 50 meters before the 10 km mark. This was fuelling my drive. I finally got passed him and noticed his age was well over 75. He is a great example of what to strive for as I get older. As I endured on I could see some folks ahead, I finally felt part of the race. Now remember I was doing a 3:30 race pace and was zipping past tons of people and each group would chatter the same thing, "Wow, where did he come from?" or "Does he know how much is left?" and occasionally some would holler "Show off!". I did have some occasions to EXPLAIN that I started an HOUR late, and to my amazement some of the runners would comment, yes we saw you running the other way at the beginning. Then they would offer some encouraging words, and off I would go to overtake the next pack.

Well I crossed the ½ way mark just over 1 hour 31 minutes and kept pushing hard. I did not let up the pedal, the whole time.

I continued passing a lot of people and kept up the pace. The rapid pace was beginning to have its effects on my body. I could no longer feel my right foot; I have consumed copious amounts of Gatorade up my nose, eyes and every other place except my mouth of course. Approaching the finishing stretch the power of the crowds kicked in and I felt energized. I remember passing Lansdowne Park, my mental marker to know that if I made it here I would have no problem finishing. I saw the 38 km marker. In fact I am not too sure which came first. Things are a bit hazy during this part of the race. I looked at my watch and the time was 2:50; that meant that I had 20 minutes to complete the last 4 km and qualify for the Boston Marathon. I thought long and hard about giving the last final push. I kept my pace and crossed the line at 3 hrs 14 minutes with my "victory pose." The official time was 4 hrs 05 minutes.

Next time I will make sure to read my race manual. See you all in Boston eventually.

Arthur now lives in Wakefield, Quebec. He is a father of two and is a software manager. He has done more races and has not been to Boston, yet.

Shaunene Neilson

Shaunene Neilson

■ *"Stupid hill! What sadist puts a hill on mile 23/24 of a marathon?"*

Shaunene Neilson, Lions Bay, BC runs the marathon by herself. She is not without the support of her family. This is for them! Overcoming moments of despair fuels her confidence to do this once again!

Marathon, hmmmm, interesting idea but no, I do not think so. Followed by: Why is a pit bull chasing me?

I always thought that only true athletes, elite runners or the slightly off centre could or would do marathons and whenever I met someone who had completed one, I was in awe.

As a runner, the furthest I had ever gone was 10K, and I was not consistent with my running. Sometimes I would run 5x a week for a month and then I would become distracted and do something else.

This is my commentary on my journey, and while I may not be an elite runner and only a so so athlete, I have been told I may be slightly off centre.

I am now standing at the start line of the marathon. Oh my god, what am I doing?!? Breathe in, breathe out. I tell myself not to cry because 4,000 people are singing the national anthem. I need to stay hydrated. I am with my pace bunny and that's a good thing, right?

He is going a little quicker than I would like and we have a long way to go. Bye bunny! Okay, that's better. I found my rhythm. Keep this for 23 more miles. I can still see the bunny so it is all good. I am going to do a negative split. Everyone says that all the best runners in the world do negative splits, so that is what I am going to do.

Wow, there goes the leader! There is the first woman! Go girl Go! Girl power! I high five a female stranger beside me!

I feel good. I feel strong, and I wonder how everyone else is doing. I am feeling a little lonely. I know it is my first marathon and I should not focus on my time. But gosh, right now, I really think I can do it in 4:30 - 4:35!

Halfway there and into the park we go! ED! Thanks for coming out to cheer.

Over the hill and down the road to English Bay we go. Downhill, yeah!

Bring on the bridge!!! Mile 17 no problem! I can do anything now!

Kits Beach, and it is only mile 22! No there must be a misprint! It can't be. Someone get the correct sign out here.

Nice well-meaning lady on the side of the road says: "You are almost there, you can do it."

No I am not, almost there, I still have 4 miles to go. Does she know how far 4 miles is?!?

My legs feel like lead and I only have one gel left (sigh). Well 5 hours is still a respectable time to finish. It is my first marathon after all and I must keep going forward.

Under the bridge and up the hill to the %#$@# bridge. Stupid hill! What sadist puts a hill on mile 23/24 of a marathon? Hills are our friends. That is what Paul always says. Guess what Paul? This hill is NOT my friend. Place one foot in front of the other; there you go, the hill is done.

Beep, beep beep, walk break. Should I take it? No, better not. I am a little worried I may not start again. Almost at the end of the bridge, slow and easy, that's all I need to do. Go to your happy place.

Home stretch and am I tired, toying with the idea of walking. Joe! It is at times like that I remember why I fell in love with my partner. Joe, who had trained so hard and heartbreakingly had an injury 2 weeks before the race. He came out with one of my nieces and ran with me for the last mile. He assured me that I had done a fabulous job and that he was proud of me. This was my moment and it was all about me. On the contrary, it was about him, the rest of my family, my running friends, and my coach. This was my tribute to them for always believing in me, even when I was not sure. They would pop up at the right moment to guide and support me on the journey.

Crossing the finish line was pure relief at 4 hours 51 minutes. But then the pain, oh the pain. Why oh why did I ever do this! NEVER AGAIN.

It's the next morning and I am a little stiff. I come into the kitchen and Joe smiles and shakes his head as I am saying... "So I was thinking, maybe with some core training I can improve my time to 4:30 for the next one."

Marathon...sure why not? I may not be an elite runner and only a so so athlete, but it is confirmed, I am most definitely a little off centre.

Shaunene has always played sports. She considers herself a true running addict. Since the above marathon she has completed several 21.1K races, and another marathon finishing in 4:33 She has finished a half-iron man Triathlon in anticipation of eventually doing Ironman in 2009. In her running circles she is fondly nicknamed the "hill Nazi"! Her next adventure is captain of a relay team for an 80km Trail race - The Squamish Stormy.

Photo courtesy of Chris Laundry

Louise Rachlis

■ *"A very fast marathon runner has told me he thought it must be harder for me than for him because I'm out on the course for so long."*

Louise Rachlis, from Ottawa, Ontario reminds us that it is never too late to start running. We can indeed take control of our lives and have fun with it. The best runners never take themselves too seriously. They just get it done. I love that about this story.

I was buying my annual pair of two-layer running socks, and the young clerk asked me if I was doing any races at the upcoming National Capital Race Weekend.

"I'm doing the marathon again," I said.

"Was it fun last year?" she chirped.

Fun?!

"A marathon is not fun," I replied.

Fun?! I'm now up to eight marathons, and it gets harder, not easier.

When I saw that the Penguin's column in Runner's World is now titled "No Need for Speed", I was similarly dismayed.

Don't you think we'd go faster if we could? Of course, there's a need. If I could finish sooner, I would. Most of us at the back of the pack are going as fast as we can.

Fun? Running downhill is fun. Biking with a tailwind is fun. Swimming in salt water is fun. I need all the gravity-assisted help I can get.

As I run, I go up and down my body, monitoring my physical distractions from top to bottom - sweat in eyes, sniffy nose, chapped lips, sore throat, heartburn, stiff, sore knees, sore left calf, arches and balls of feet calloused, blistered toes - and that's just what I'll tell you about!

Then there's the mental, usually related to the fact that I'm the slowest human on the Rideau Canal, and I don't have time for this.

My daughter Diana tells me her mantra to keep going when she runs is "Mommy and size 6." I thought that was pretty good, so I began to tell myself "Diana and size 6" when I was faltering. But for me, one mantra isn't enough. It takes me so long to finish that I need dozens of 'em.

One thing I do is imagine my two favorite fast runners, each holding me up, one lifting each arm, like angels.

I also talk to myself in various ways, repeating for instance, "Look at me, I'm nice and light, and I've just begun to fight." It isn't deep, but it works.

I try to focus on what parts of my body are working - such as breathing well - rather than my swollen feet, sore back or chafing thighs.

During the half marathon, I tell myself, 'if you don't do this, how can you do a marathon?'

In the marathon, I remind myself I'm getting closer to my decade goal of 10 marathons by the time I'm 60. Part of the problem is I'm getting slower so I'm out there longer, working just as hard. I tell myself, slow running is better than no running.

A very fast marathon runner has told me he thought it must be harder for me than for him because I'm out on the course for so long.

I'm sure he was just being kind, but the recognition of the special needs of slow runners was appreciated.

When I ran my first marathon in 1999, I mentioned to a co-worker that I was afraid there wouldn't be any fruit left in the food tent by the time I got in.

He handed me a banana over the fence just before the finish line, and so my "official" finish line photo looks as if I ran 26.2 miles while carrying a banana.

Running is not easy. Everyone competing on the race weekend has worked hard and deserves congratulations for their efforts. So, fast and slow, good for all of us!

Since turning 50... ten years ago, Louise has learned to run marathons, cycle long distances, cross country ski and swim in open water. She looks forward to seeing what adventures the next decade will bring. When she's not training for triathlons, watercolor painting, travelling, or thinking about writing fiction, she works as Advertising Features Editor at the Ottawa Citizen.

Photo courtesy of Chris Laundry

Ellen Roseman

■"Finding fans to cheer you on is crucial to marathon success, too. You're advised to recruit the help of strangers along the route by writing your name on your clothes or legs."

Ellen Roseman, from Toronto, Ontario gives us a formula for financing our marathons, in case we decide to run them every year. She offers practical, sensible, advice. Sure put a smile on my face....

Marathons offer lessons on running your life.

I'm going to write about how training for a marathon prepares you for other gruelling assignments, such as organizing your finances or managing your career.

Some people are not fans of long-distance running or the middle-aged women who "simply look ridiculous" doing it.

Well, here's a news flash. Slow-paced strolling won't make you fit. Fitness is one reason we "hard-nosed columnists" have embraced marathons. But it's not the only thing that keeps us going.

I had plenty of time - six hours, in fact - to ponder the attraction as I competed in, and completed, the Marine Corps Marathon in Washington, D.C. last Sunday. What follows are lessons on what marathon training can teach you about business and life.

Set your sights high.

Failure is a constant possibility, no matter what you do to improve your economic status. You can start an investment program just before the stock market tanks. Or you can embark on a new career and miss the signs the sector is shaky.

Guesswork is part of any long-term venture, so you're always staring failure in the face. Get used to it.

When it comes to marathon training, you can spend months to get in shape - only to lose your preparation to a last-minute injury. But at least you had a noble goal, a vision of success that made it all worthwhile. You risked a lot and lost, but you didn't dream on a small scale.

If you're going to fail anyway, fail big.

Train properly.

You can't get from here to there without a plan. I'm talking about a detailed plan that takes your noble goal and breaks it into manageable and easy-to-digest chunks.

Suppose you want to retire with $2 million in your RRSP. Posting a sign on your fridge isn't enough. You need a financial planner - or financial planning software - to tell you how much to save each month (and at what investment return) to get you to the $2 million mark.

As your income grows and you get used to living with less, you can add more dollars to your monthly savings plan.

That's how marathon training works. You start with the idea of running 26.2 miles, but you can't reach the end of your block without getting winded. So, you run five minutes in comfort, then try 10 minutes next week and 20 minutes the week after that. You add the minutes - and the miles - more quickly as your tolerance grows.

Don't hit the wall.

Some marathon runners collapse at 20 to 21 miles, about three-quarters of the way through the course. They walk the rest or give up altogether.

Hitting the wall can result from not pacing yourself, starting too fast and flaming out.

Distance runners start slowly and don't get anxious if they seem to fall behind. They conserve the energy to power them through the last few miles.

So, too, with business. Although sprints are required along the way, the key to success is a long-term perspective -

patience, fortitude, resilience, sustainability - ahead of the short-distance vision and quick-burn.

Hire a cheering section.

It's hard to be brave and stoic on your own. You're more likely to stay the course if you're surrounded by friendly folks who support what you're doing.

When it comes to saving, this means getting family and friends on track. You can't put money away for the future if they're intent on spending it all today. When it comes to starting your own business, this means getting employees to sing from the same song sheet. Either they breathe the mission or they breeze out the door.

Finding fans to cheer you on is crucial to marathon success too. You're advised to recruit the help of strangers along the route by writing your name on your clothes or legs.

My mantra, "Go Ellen", printed in red marker on my T-shirt, was picked up and repeated by thousands of onlookers. It was electrifying to be the recipient of so much good will.

Control what you can.

In a marathon, you can't do anything about the weather. (Ours was hot and humid and always on the verge of rain.) You can't do anything about the jostling crowds of runners or the route.

But you can control your thoughts. Instead of dwelling on what's wrong and holding you back, think of how you'll make it to the end and how great you'll feel when you're done.

That's the mentality you need to succeed in your career or in any long-term venture. Focus on what's within your power to control and you'll feel free and have a sense of autonomy. And isn't that what life's all about?

Ellen is a personal finance and consumer affairs columnist with the Toronto Star. She is the author of several books, and teaches courses on investing.

Photo courtesy of Carl Wagar

■ Tough times
don`t last, tough
people do.

~ *Anonymous*

Jennifer Sharpe

■ *"The*
American
anthem
played, the
fireworks
went off, and
I crossed the
Start line,
and I was
living my
dream. "

"A dream is a wish your heart makes. " This is what Jennifer Sharpe, from Coquitlam, British Columbia makes us believe. Surrounding yourself with those who believe you can do it is the key to any endeavour. It makes for a memorable read.

How many people actually get to live their dream?

It was in 2004 that I started to dream of running my first marathon, and I wanted it to be at Walt Disney World in Florida. I'd only just started running, and a marathon was so unreachable! How was I going to do this? Lucky for me, I'm not just a dreamer. I'm a do-er. And when I want something, I get it.

And I wanted to live my dream.

None of my friends were planning to run this event. I was on my own training for my first marathon, but soon I came to realize that I wasn't on my own because I'd spent the past 3 years telling everyone what my dream was, that Disney would be my first marathon! And before I knew it, runners and friends were offering their time and support to help me live my dream. My friend Karen is my greatest hero. Karen ran the last 10-12-k of every single long run with me. Without fail, she showed up. We had our coldest winter in 31 years in Vancouver, BC. I trained through record setting snowfalls, rainfalls and cold temperatures. We had numerous power outages and hurricane-force wind storms. Karen still showed up, even through all the complaints and whining. She never failed. I couldn't have done it without her.

I got to race day on Sunday January 7, 2007. Oh my goodness, I can't believe it's here! The American anthem played, the fireworks went off, and I crossed the Start line, and I was living my dream. How did I get to be so lucky?

All the Disney characters lined the route, and I carried my camera. I posed with every single character along the way. I high-fived Pluto; I flew with Peter Pan and Wendy; I ran down Main Street USA and ran through Cinderella's castle; I touched a 22 year old turtle in the Animal Kingdom. Disney thinks of everything.

It was a tough event. I've never had anything take everything out of me. At mile 24 something happened that I never want to experience again. I quit. I've never quit anything in my life that I worked so hard to get. My body, mind and spirit quit. But then I met an angel. I heard a voice, a gentleman yell,"Way to go Canada; where are you from?" And I burst into tears. He pulled me aside to tell me that I could do it! I had it in me to go the last 2 miles and finish what I'd started. He said it was all about the mind, but my mind was strong and I would finish. I don't know who that man was. I don't know his name or even what he looked like. But if not for him, I would not have finished. Those last 2 miles were for him. He helped me make my dream come true, and how can I thank him when I don't know who he is? Thank you my angel, kind sir. You'll never know what you helped to do.

I had the privilege of meeting John "The Penguin" Bingham while at the Disney expo, and he said something that really stuck with me. He talked about setting time goals, and clearly said not to. This was Disney! Why rush through it, he said. Go slow and savour every moment of it. Don't wish that it will end....wish that it won't. I've thought long and hard about the entire day, and I'm so happy that I made it an all day event. I was training to complete in 5:30, and for 2 days after the race, I cried because it took me so much longer. I felt like I'd failed because I hadn't met my time goal. But now I'm so happy that it took me longer. I have all those memories that I wouldn't have had if I'd been faster. I wouldn't have the 75 pictures I took. The time doesn't matter because my dream came true.

I've wondered over and over why I'm so lucky that my dream came true. So many people wish for it, but for me, it happened. Well, I know how it happened. I not only dreamed my dream; I did something about it. I made it happen. I dared to dream something really big, and it came true because I wanted it to. That's why I'm so lucky. Success happened because I finished a big event like a marathon through tough odds. I doubted afterwards whether I could call myself a marathoner, but I am a marathoner. And I'm not just any marathoner. A marathoner who made her dream come true. Nothing is better than that.

Jennifer works in the wine industry. She started running along with her 11yr common law spouse as part of a weight loss challenge. She has run in many races and is planning her 2nd marathon. Running gives her purpose. Every run teaches her a truth about herself she didn't know before. Running has changed her life.

■ "Every survival
kit should include
a sense of humour"

~ *Anonymous*

Elizabeth Sleen

Elizabeth Sleen, from Victoria, B.C. finds a part of herself she never knew existed, and in doing so, understands her world around her. It is a better place to be.

■ *"Although probably not meant as encouragement or even for me to overhear, those were some of the most inspirational words I've ever heard"*

The date itself is inconsequential.

When I think back to that weekend we spent in Tofino, it is the details that I treasure. Details like the pre-race pasta and salmon dinner complete with shell decorations beautifully laid out on the tables. Details like the delicious chocolate desserts donated by local hotels, and my son playing in the sand on the beach and knowing that I would be running on that same beach the next morning in my first marathon.

I have a thousand tiny memories that swirl around that race but not one of them is of the date or my pacing or the time it took me to finish. Those are the details I thought would be important; those are not the ones I value.

In the year before I decided to run my first marathon, my life changed in more ways than it stayed the same: I met and married my husband, we moved across the country, I started a new job and we had a baby. Happy changes all of them, but unsettling changes none the less. I was happy in my role as wife and mother, but I did not feel grounded. I needed a goal towards which to work and I wanted to do something for myself, which is partly why I chose to run a marathon.

I met my husband a few days after he finished his first marathon. At that time I ran, but only for fun and a marathon existed only on the periphery of my consciousness.

My attempts to impress him with 5K runs only made his eyes glaze over and I realized I wanted to understand the importance that running had for him.

My first race was a 10K through the Don Valley during a torrential downpour. Pregnancy sidetracked my plans to run a half-marathon. Before the birth of our son, my husband ran two more marathons. I met him at the finish line, prepared with snacks, sandals, cooling gels and water. I was still confused yet attempting to understand the passion that fuelled his intensity for running.

It was part curiosity and part selfishness that inspired me to sign up for the Edge 2 Edge marathon from Tofino to Ucluelet. My initial fears about completing the training with my then 7 month old son strapped into the jogging stroller proved to be unfounded. Before I started I had unspoken goals: to prove to myself and to others that I could physically do this and that I could see a project through to completion. What I hadn't expected were the little lessons I learned along the way: to be forgiving of myself when I missed a run, the pride I felt when I did my runs, and to be patient when my son didn't nap but needed to walk along the side of the path.

I also found a tremendous sense of accomplishment. On race day, support from the expected and unexpected reinforced how much running this marathon meant to me. I strained my eyes looking for the distant figures of my husband and son standing by the side of the road to cheer me on. Toward the end of the race, once the adrenaline and novelty had worn off, the words from my friend that "it's only running for four hours; it's actually pretty awful," had never sounded more true. I passed a water station and heard one of the volunteers say, "She's a marathoner. I saw her at the start line." Me, they were talking about me: a marathoner! Although probably not meant as encouragement or even for me to overhear, those were some of the most inspirational words I've ever heard.

More memories flood my thoughts of the race: the man sitting on the side of the path, unable to run any further; the woman running next to me who keeps pushing me to keep going a little further; suddenly coming around the corner to cross the finish line under the balloon arch; hugging my husband

and son; collapsing on the grass. The race is over, but I have more than a race bib and medal around my neck. I am proud of finishing. I understand why my husband has run three marathons. I am proud of the example I've set for my son.

As the one-year anniversary of my first marathon looms closer I have a different understanding of what I gained from crossing the finish line that day. I had been waiting for the moment when I could define myself apart from wife and mother. I wanted the results, and pictures and medal as testimony of what I had accomplished. As I stood at the start line, I realized that moment had come. But as the kilometres slipped under my feet, I became conscious of the fact that although this was my race, I was not then, nor had I ever been alone on this journey. And more importantly, I did not want to be alone as I neared the end. It wasn't fear or a belief that I could not finish, but an overwhelming need to share this milestone with those who had encouraged me from the moment I signed up.

Here is what I know. The hard work it took to reach my goal gave me security. I am not eclipsed by being a wife or mother - I am enriched. All the joy I felt crossing the finish line that day was doubled because of the two people waiting on the other side.

Elizabeth works as an army reservist. She is presently a stay at home mom to her 2yr old son and is expecting a 2nd child soon. She has plans to run in the future. She is thankful for her Sister-in-law's inspiration.

Photo courtesy of Gavin Lumsden, Berlin Marathon

Stephanie Sleen

■ *"I think I have found a sport that will follow me throughout my life, this definitely won't be my last. "*

Stephanie Sleen, from Calgary, Alberta, imparts her words of wisdom in the telling of her story on running her first marathon. We can all learn from her.

I am 35,000 feet high, both literally and figuratively. I'm in a plane flying over the ocean to Maui, Hawaii to reach the end of an eight month journey of struggle, hard work and persistence.

I'm on my way to run my first marathon. People always say that the destination is not the important part of a dream; it's the journey to get there that makes the difference. Many runners would disagree. They would say the finish line is the most important part of a marathon goal. I think you learn a lot about yourself on the journey to get to that finish line. For me, training seemed to be further than 42.2km (26.2miles) away.

Back in January I decided to run the Maui Marathon. My reasons back then were a lot different than they are today. I wanted a challenge, I wanted to test my endurance and I wanted to be a part of the small percentage of the world who has actually crossed the finish line of a marathon. My training took me through many emotions, challenges, aches and pains, triumphs and failures. There were good training days, and training runs that ended in tears and disappointment. But I learned something from every one of those runs. About half way to my ultimate goal, I ran the Vancouver half marathon and finished respectably.

I was half way to the marathon in both time and distance. The closer the marathon date got, the more it seemed to be a trivial goal after all those miles of training. Trivial or not, I would finish the marathon to prove that it could be done and it could be done by someone like me.

The plan was pretty clear up until three days ago when my father passed away of Shy-Dragger Syndrome (a rare form of Parkinson's disease). He struggled so hard in the last few months he lived; he struggled way harder than I ever had in any run. To lose your Dad when you are only twenty-three years old is something that is very hard to deal with. I had less than a week to decide what to do about the marathon. Should I run it or not?

Everything I have ever read about marathon training says to avoid stress the week before the race at all cost. This was about as stressful as it gets. I decided to run the race for my Dad. He was proud of me that I was going to run it and he would have been devastated that I didn't run it on his account.

So that brings me to where I am today, flying to achieve something great in honor of my Dad. I just want to finish the race for him, that would be an achievement in itself. Dreams do change with time, and this marathon has become more important to me than ever before.

It's the morning of September 22, the day after the race and I'm in bed paralyzed with an unbelievable amount of pain. But it is a pain of satisfaction and success. It's a pain that few have had the opportunity to achieve. I crossed the finish line four hours and fifteen minutes after the start. It was four hours and fifteen minutes of the most incredible ups and downs I have ever had emotionally and physically. It's definitely true that this race is more about your mental attitude than your physical ability. The camaraderie along the way was phenomenal, the way the runners pulled each other along the way through the mental struggles. The final 6.2 miles took all I had emotionally and physically, I think my Dad was looking over me that final stretch because there were points that I really don't know how I kept going. The heat was unbearable (92 degrees Fahrenheit at the finish line) and many people went down without finishing.

It was hard to see someone lose their dream so close to the finish. The pain will eventually go away but the memory of every second of that 26.2 miles will always be with me. As well as the memory of the unbelievable pride that came over the faces of everyone crossing the finish line. Everyone runs a marathon for different reasons. That day I ran for my Dad. I think I have found a sport that will follow me throughout my life, this definitely won't be my last. But I will never forget my first marathon in Maui that I did for my Dad.

Stephanie is living in Alaska doing backcountry trips with youth at risk. She is nearly finished her divemaster training in Honduras. She hopes to start training for an ironman soon.

Photo courtesy of Phil Marsh

David Stewart

David Stewart from Calgary, Alberta is the kind of runner who embraces speed and makes his dream come true.

■ *"I did have to avoid a peacock near the exit and I am sure that there are not many races that can say that peacocks can be an obstacle to overcome. "*

Just before I turned 41, I ran the Calgary marathon - I was still 40 and it was the 40th running of the race so for my "one and only marathon" it just worked. I had way too much fun and ran it in a little under 4 hours. In the days following that race I got it stuck in my head, that with better training, I could make Boston.

I ran two half marathons in the fall and the results were encouraging. In December, I started to train for the July Calgary marathon. My one and only goal of 3:20, was the time I needed to qualify for Boston.

After building a very good base through a lot of miles, a lot of days plus gym work, I switched to 3 - 4 days a week of high intensity running. Ran a half marathon in the spring with great results but ... it was a half.

The week leading up to the marathon itself was filled with self-doubt.

What was I thinking running so hard for so long during my training runs? I had to do more, there was no way I was ready I thought to myself. Slowly but surely I regained my composure and steadied myself for the race.

It was a cool start, around 6 C. The first klick was text book - nice and easy running at a 4:50 km pace. I slowly increased the pace as we ran through the Stampede grounds. It was Kids day so there was always the threat of a parent running across our paths but I did not experience any problems.

Got behind two grey beards that seemed to be setting a good pace so I did not even look at my watch. As we ran through the Calgary Zoo I overheard them saying they were running a 4:30 km pace. The Zoo would have been neat but now I was into full running concentration mode - hat pulled down, head slightly bent forward and focused on the running and so I was out of the Zoo before I saw much. I did have to avoid a peacock near the exit and I am sure that there are not many races that can say that peacocks can be an obstacle to overcome.

I ran up the "big" hill with good form. At the crest, the city center with the Rocky Mountains behind on a clear morning did make a great sight. Another runner attempted to make some conversation with me but my plan was to run my own race and his stride did not match mine so that ended very quickly.

I thought I was making good time - the strategy was to aim for 3:17 so that there was room for error near the end should my stride fail. At the half way mark, I should have been 1:38:30 but was now 1:39:00. No time to panic but also no time to start to take it easy. The legs felt strong. I did not miss a water station and the three gels already in my system seemed to be doing the trick.

Slowly but surely I picked up the pace which resulted in a rather weird feeling. There were now times where the runner in front of me was a minute or two ahead and no one behind me in sight - we were now running through a residential area with winding roads.

A couple of more gels and a quick stop at the water stations for one water, one Gatorade and the pace is very doable.

At the 25K mark I am one minute behind the schedule but have been there for a couple of clicks. Start to bare down as I am feeling good and now is the time to make up ground - a slight downhill. A small steep down hill and around

Bowness Park and then the next thing I know I am at the 30K mark.

Mental fatigue. Not a good time to attempt to figure out the pace one needs to run 5.2K in 25 minutes or less. Or was it 24 minutes, damn, I forgot.

Put your head down and run your own race. Continue to pass other runners. "Good running" they yell out as I pass. "You too" is all I can manage to mumble back.

Throw water in the vicinity of my mouth, the sponges are great, squeeze them over my back. One mile to go but my mind is mush. Who cares, run you dumb bastard, run. Where is that finish line? My mind is now completely numb. A couple of hundred meters to go, the legs are starting to give out, right calf is cramping. So I do what any sane person would do, I start to sprint. So much for the head up, hands raised in victory, now I am in survival mode - do whatever to end this and get across the finish line.

I hear my name. I hear the time called - confirmed. I have run the marathon in 3:16:59. I am going to Boston!

David Stewart has run Boston several times now and he claims his supportive wife always asks him if this is the last one.....

Photo courtesy of Angelo Talluto

Angelo Talluto

■ *"I don't know what that feeling or vision was, but I do know that it was responsible for taking my soul to a place that it had never been. I ran for 41K but floated for 1.2."*

Angelo Talluto from Toronto, Ontario sent this story at the very early stages of having launched our website. It became the story which kept inspiring me of the power of one.

I was a 30 year old, healthy, athletic male, newlywed teacher, with a wonderful wife who was seven months pregnant. Things were great. The next day, my profile changed. In a matter of hours, the doctors, one being my friend Dave, had determined that I had a large brain tumour that has been slowly growing for 8-10 years. My profile was now a 30-year-old, newlywed male with a wonderful pregnant wife, and a brain tumour.

Surgery happened a month later. The days in the hospital were horrible. I remember each minute, hour, and day I spent there. I particularly remember a strange moment that happened to me in the middle of the night. I lay in my hospital bed, with no one around, my head between my knees, and cried. I took a deep breath, looked up, and saw white. White is the only way to put it in words. It was more of a feeling, a sense of hope and direction, but also one of confusion. What was it? Why was I feeling this way? The next thing I know, my nurse comes into my room and wakes me up.

Confused as can be, I dismissed it, figuring it was the medication playing tricks on my mind. I regained feeling in my arm and my rehab began to show some progress.

After a severely depressing month of August, September came around, and things began to change. My son was born on the 27th and rehab was looking good. It lasted until November when I was diagnosed with Classic K.S, a rare type of skin Cancer. I had surgery again to remove a few tumours on my foot, but this time, instead of falling into depression again, I became desperate and obsessed with doing whatever I could do to make this go away. Running a marathon was my answer.

I can't really say why I picked a marathon, but it seemed the most extreme way of distracting me. Completing an extreme physical challenge within one year of my surgery may be the inspiration my family might long for if ever they needed it. People thought I was crazy, especially with the medication I was on. I thought it was necessary.

I signed up for the Ottawa marathon in May. I did everything possible to make sure I was ready. Although we never ran together, my friend Dave decided to run it as well. Time was not an issue while I was training. I was only concerned with finishing. My training had a few bumps in the road (no pun intended), but I made it to the start.

The gun goes, and I kept questioning myself: "Why am I here?" What am I doing? I began to run and continuously questioned my sanity. The 4:15 Pace Bunny was working out well until I had to go to the washroom. By the time I got back on the road, the 4:15 was out of sight. I debated what to do, and then decided to chase him. I finally got to him a few km later. I began to wonder how close I was to the 4hr Bunny. I asked someone in the crowd and they said he just passed. I thought of how much better, and wonderful, it would be to achieve my first marathon under 4 hrs and became obsessed with catching him. I figured if I could catch up to the 4:15 after the washroom break, then I can catch the 4 hr PB easily. I asked again, and one gentleman said just over a minute. Every time I asked someone, they would tell me that I was closer and closer.

The half way mark came and went quickly. I saw my wife and boy and it just made me want that 4hr bunny even more. By 27K I began running behind a man who seemed to look like Dave. Once I got closer, I realized who it was and almost tackled him. Dave's eyes almost popped out when he saw me and I was so happy to see him!! Throughout my surgery, Dave was so supportive and always made me feel strong. He did the same during the race. I felt great.

At 33K, I was still obsessed by the 4hr bunny, and I told Dave I wanted 4hrs, and looking at how good I looked, he pushed me forward to go get him. A woman beside me also had the same intentions, so we ran together, supporting each other to catch this guy.

At 36K, we asked again, and someone screamed out "100 meters!" We knew we had him. Just a little bit to go, and then it happened. I now know why it's called hitting the wall. All of a sudden, I had nothing. I looked at the woman and told her to go get him. She went, and I broke down in tears. I thought the race was over. I lost 4 hrs. My legs were hurting, I felt dizzy, and my body was pleading with me to stop, but I knew it wasn't an option. This horrible year would not end without that finish line.

Dave caught up at 40K and was surprised to see me in that condition. I knew he wanted to stay with me, but I pushed him along. This was my journey to take, and I had to take it alone.

At 41K, it seemed that it was over for me, but then all of a sudden, it happened. Thousands of people were watching, screaming and waving their arms frantically in support of all the runners, and I didn't even notice. I lifted my sunglasses to wipe the tears, and once I opened my eyes, the feeling came back: I was seeing white again, nothing else, just white. That familiar feeling was back and It carried me 1200 meters to the finish line.

I don't know what that feeling or vision was, but I do know that it was responsible for taking my soul to a place that it had never been. I ran for 41K, but floated for 1.2.

The last 10 seconds before finishing was my countdown to the end of this year. I enter this New Year with a new profile: A strong 31 yr old father, husband, Cancer survivor, and Marathon runner.

Photo courtesy of Angelo Talluto

Angelo is a husband & father of 2 boys, and a grade 4 teacher. He has recently lost his father to cancer. For the second time in his life, a tragedy has made him a stronger person.

"Each time I do go out, I remember the journey that I've taken to get to where I am today and it always makes me want to sprint the last kilometer home."

Fred van der Gaag

Chosen words fuel the brain, much like a power gel can do to your body. Words work for Fred van der Gaag, from Kelowna, B.C.

■ *"Then...*
nearing the
top of the
climb, a
young man
was holding
a sign high
above him
that read
"Believe in
Your Self"

It was everything I expected and more, much more. This was one of the most exciting, most emotional events that I've ever been involved in.

On Saturday afternoon we walked down to the Marathon Expo to pick up our race kits and look around at the different booths. We lucked out and happened to be there when Running Room owner John Stanton gave an excellent, uplifting speech. Shortly after I bought his book, chatted briefly with this fine gentleman and asked him to autograph it. He wrote, "To Fred, First Marathon...you can do it!"

On race day morning, strangely enough I didn't feel all that nervous, just excited and a little anxious but also healthy and fit.

I had many strong feelings while waiting for the gun. They played "One Moment in Time" by Whitney Houston which I used to think was a corny, silly song but at that moment it was perfect and stirring. Watching the people around me I saw raw emotion and a few tears. I was welling up a bit myself... after all the months of training, after all the miles ran in preparation, after not drinking any of my beloved beer since January 1st I was finally here, at the start of my first and maybe only marathon. Then the count down to the gun began and the race was on. I took off feeling great but my right hip began to hurt a lot shortly after. I worried about this a bit but the pain went away after 5k or so. Off came my "rain jacket". My breathing was a little laboured till around the 10k mark, which is normal for me. I ditched the sweatshirt about an hour into it, which was an indication of how cold it was. I didn't remove it because I was hot, it was just getting too wet and heavy from the rain. I was running smooth through the city, the first crossing of the Burard Bridge and the Gastown stretch. We came into Stanley Park and started up Prospect Pt. Hill, which is the hardest.

I began running again, up the ramp on to Burard Bridge for the last time. Somehow the steepness of the ramp had increased dramatically from the previous two times I crossed the damned bridge! I'm now feeling

lonely and scared and I knew that I was teetering on the edge. I had always believed that I would finish; it was just a matter of how fast. Now I wasn't so sure. The people cheering on the side of the bridge were fantastic. Where before the spectators seemed to be looking at other runners, now they seemed to be looking at me...I guess they tend to focus on the runners with the haunted look on their faces! The words I heard most were "you can do it" and I remembered what John Stanton wrote on my book. Then...nearing the top of the climb, a young man was holding a sign high above him that read "Believe in Your Self". This was an incredible mental and emotional boost. I tried to say "thanks man" or something like that but not much more than a grunt is what came out. Then, only 2k left, all flat. I looked up and saw a runner in front of me wearing a shirt that had the seven stages of the marathon written on the back. I read the list. Ritual, Shock, Denial, Isolation when I got to the fifth stage "Despair" I understood exactly what it meant. I guess I must have said it out loud when I thought, "I know at which stage I am in right now" as a couple of runners beside me laughed. Then I smiled too because I knew I was going to make it. The last two stages are; Affirmation and Renewal...they would come.

I could hear the music and cheering coming from the finish line. Then, there it was, that beautiful finish sign with the balloons over it... I pulled myself up as straight as I could and tried my best not to limp. I would cross that finish line looking like a runner and not just any runner...I was a marathoner.

So, I didn't get my time. Perhaps the running gods don't approve of first timers getting their way so easy. That's ok; I learned much about my body, my mind and my spirit. 3:32:59 is what my official time was and I'm very happy with it. I'm also very happy with an incredible thought that I had somewhere along those very painful last 5k, it was... "I want to do this again; I want to run another marathon!" I will.

Since this marathon, Fred has run 10 more, and ran Boston in 2006. He is a father of two sons, and has 2 grandchildren. Since he started running he has lost about 30 lbs. He is healthier, fitter, and at 46 yrs of age, a whole lot happier. Last year, he completed his first IronMan in Penticton. He is working at breaking the 3 hr barrier in the marathon. He continues to reside in Kelowna with his girlfriend, and running partner Heather.

■ Our greatest
weakeness lies in
giving up. The
most certain way
to succeed is always
to try just one
more time.

~ *Thomas Edison*

Linda Rainville Wagar

■ *"Think of all the people who can't, won't or don't have this incredible experience. For all those who never have, and all the people who never will, on your own terms, and at your own pace....just GET IT DONE!"*

I am calm and confident once I get on the bus that takes me to Buffalo N.Y, the start line of the Niagara Falls Marathon. For now it is drizzling and the winds are light; later, the overcast skies made running my third 42.2K race, the best ever.

For me, this marathon is all about experiencing the people I meet along the way, some in flesh and some conjured in my mind. Each and every one of them will be responsible for my crossing the finish line.

I see the man from Finland. He told me yesterday "This is my 130th Marathon." He runs effortlessly for a man I judge to be in his 60's. Later, I will check his time and discover he has won in his age category.

I run behind a guy with crooked legs and an unusual gait. What a strange but surprisingly fast way of running. I finally catch up to him only to lose him again at the 10th kilometer when I greet my spectator husband enroute. Ultimately, it is the crooked man I run behind for much of the first half of the race and he inspires me to run faster.

Along the route, casual conversations pass the time. I run my own race and never speak with anyone for too long, except with the guy wearing "Thanks, Jen" on his shirt who looks to be twenty-something. I see him often and build up the courage to ask: "Are you going to ask Jen to marry you?" He smiles, "I already did, maybe I will again!"

A young spectator, shouts: "It doesn't matter if you are first or last, you are all winners for crossing that finish!" His big brown eyes show a grateful and surprised look when I yell back. "You are awesome to say that!! Thanks so much!!"

The Emergency Medics on bicycles keep a close watch on us, especially after the 25K mark. One medic tells me, "You look strong, you are going to be fine, and the last part of this race is going to be just fine!".

He verbalizes what I know and confirm to myself: I now have 30K behind me and yes! I feel in control. I have been passing people, fully expecting to see them again, but never do. Never have I passed so many people in a race before! My goal is to feel strong at this point in the journey and I am well on my way!

When I stop for water at 34K, the next thing I know, I am crying. Crying? I have never cried while racing. Suddenly, I feel broken. A volunteer tells me "Don't cry, there's only 8K to go!". What's happening? I realize I have no tears and take this as a sign that I must be dehydrated. I drink more water and with fragile determination, I resume my run.

I think of my training partners in Ottawa, rooting for me, in spirit. Oh, I'm so thankful that I'm here in Niagara and not running in last week's Toronto Marathon. My training partner Lilac had described her experience: "It was like I had popsicles for limbs". It gives new meaning to hell freezing over. Maybe this Niagara Falls stint isn't so bad. Keep going.

I think of Patti who is built to run marathons and remember how I marvelled at her consistency. I pretend she's still keeping pace in front, the back of her shoulders providing a focus for a tranquil trance. She is known to say "I find the hills hard". The hills are hard. She makes the training look effortless!

I think of Gavin, our group leader who made me believe in myself, telling me to run longer, faster, harder, not because I want to, but because I have it in me. He wrote our group a letter, and I remember the part about having to dig a little deeper. "Think of all the people who can't, won't or don't have this incredible experience...for all those who never have, and all the people who never will. On your own terms, and at your own pace.....just GET IT DONE!". I pretend he is running by my side.

I see a sign that says 40 K. I am nearing the end. Instead of this sign nourishing my soul, I am stopped dead in my tracks. I lose my running rhythm. I suddenly feel like a wounded animal along the side of the road, wishing I could just be put out of my misery. In a mental fog, I see my husband waving from the side of the road and I barely acknowledge him. I hate being seen this way. Although he tries to be helpful, "You are almost finished!", I feel done. Done in!

An older, wiser runner is trying to tell me to relax; "The finish is very soon, you will make it..." I make matters worse by sprinting and within a hundred meters, I can barely run on a decline portion of the road!

I know the marathon ends at the falls; and yet I can't see or hear Niagara Falls! Where is it? Where's that finish?

I see the yellow banner. "Here she comes from Ottawa, Linda Wagar, look how strong she is finishing this race!"

A woman covers me in a mylar blanket. I teeter and ask her to hold on to me. She tells someone I need medical attention. Fatigue washes over me. Yet I say, "Oh no, I just want to make sure I don't fall I want to see if I can walk alone now." Steady. I let her go, and yes! I can walk alone.

What a lovely 4 hours and 53 minute run I had today. I smile at my husband, and feel blessed.

Linda has run 4 marathons and many half marathons. She loves to encourage running! Linda is wife & mother to Sophie 12, Justin 10. She has trouble parting with her old running shoes. She enjoys planting flowers in them. Helping others cross finish lines is now a passion.

Photos courtesy of Linda Wagar

132

Acknowledgments

Thank you marathon writers for agreeing to the edited versions of your stories, and providing photos.

Thank you Emily Gildner, for inspiring me to run. You encouraged and guided me by offering editing insights for this book. Thank you Cori Slaughter, for your unwavering support.

Thank you John Stanton for igniting the belief in me that we can all run a marathon if we choose. It is a full circle moment that you agreed to become a part of this project.

Thank you Ray Zahab and Ron Wallingford for offering your reviews and your insights.

Pictures tell stories. Thank you Chris Laundry and Phil Marsh for your photos, and Cameron Wilson for your illustration.

Merci à Nathalie Collin pour ton aide avec le rassemblement d'histoires francophones; merci à Marie-Claude Côté pour ton appui.

Thank you, Lynne Bermel and Ken Parker for your participation with the book's dedication.

EntreNet Communications offered the website design, hosting, graphics, book layout & design, all gratuitously. Carl Wagar and Katharine Grace, the dream could not have happened without your touch.

To borrow from the African proverb, "It takes a village to raise a child"; it took a village to create Canadian Marathon Stories. Thank you for being a part of my village by supporting our Canadian athletes and purchasing this book.

Linda Rainville Wagar

■ Be the change
you wish to see in
the world...

~ *Gandhi*

Photo Credits

Cover design & logos EntreNet Communications Inc.

Back cover photo Chris Laundry

Photo of Linda Wagar, courtesy Chris Laundry

CAN Fund shirts on athletes courtesy Jane Roos

Photo of Emilie Mondor courtesy Bernard Brault, LaPresse

Karen Beitel, provided by Karen, Boston Marathon

Rob Bryce, taken by Rob's wife

Cameron Wilson, Illustrator of runner with wine

Nathalie Collin, Chicago Marathon, provided by Nathalie

Amanda & Mark Collis, Forest City Marathon London, provided by Mark

Tina Connelly, and Tina and Brendan Connelly, New York Road Runners Club

Robert Davidson, Boston Marathon, provided by Robert

Rosaire Gagné, provided by Rosaire

Runner in kilt, by Phil Marsh

Courage sign, by Chris Laundry

Annie Koppens, Boston Marathon, provided by Annie

Arthur Munro Ottawa Marathon, provided by Arthur

Elite runners, by Phil Marsh

Chris Fretwell, by Chris

Shaunene Neilson, provided by Shaunene

Rabbit and runners, by Chris Laundry

Runners holding hands by Chris Laundry

Jennifer Henry, provided by Jennifer

Runner on knees, by Phil Marsh

Linda Wagar, courtesy Carl Wagar

Angelo Talluto, courtesy Angelo's wife

Fred van der Gaag, provided by Fred

Middle page insert, Phil Marsh and Chris Laundry

Running shoes in bloom photos, courtesy, Linda Wagar

Margaret, 60 years-young finisher of a half marathon.
Photo courtesy of Linda Wagar